COMPUTER CODING
Games

FOR KIDS

COMPUTER CODING
Games

FOR KIDS

JON WOODCOCK
FOREWORD BY CAROL VORDERMAN

DK UK

Senior editor Ben Morgan
Project art editor Laura Brim
Editors Lizzie Davey, Ashwin Khurana, Steve Setford
Designers Mabel Chan, Peter Radcliffe, Steve Woosnam-Savage
Jacket design development manager Sophia MTT
Jacket editor Claire Gell
Producer, pre-production Francesca Wardell
Producer Mary Slater
Managing editor Paula Regan
Managing art editor Owen Peyton Jones
Publisher Andrew Macintyre
Associate publishing director Liz Wheeler
Art director Karen Self
Design director Stuart Jackman
Publishing director Jonathan Metcalf

DK DELHI

Project editor Suefa Lee
Project art editor Parul Gambhir
Editor Sonia Yooshing
Art editors Sanjay Chauhan, Upasana Sharma
Assistant art editor Simar Dhamija
Senior DTP designers Harish Aggarwal, Vishal Bhatia
Senior managing editor Rohan Sinha
Managing art editor Sudakshina Basu
Pre-production manager Balwant Singh
Jacket designer Suhita Dharamjit
Managing jackets editor Saloni Singh

First published in Great Britain in 2015
by Dorling Kindersley Limited
80 Strand, London WC2R 0RL

Copyright © 2015 Dorling Kindersley Limited
A Penguin Random House Company
2 4 6 8 10 9 7 5 3
007 – 283034 – December/2015

A CIP catalogue record for this book
is available from the British Library.
ISBN: 978-0-2412-0973-8

Printed in China

A WORLD OF IDEAS:
SEE ALL THERE IS TO KNOW

www.dk.com

CAROL VORDERMAN MA (CANTAB), MBE, is one of Britain's best-loved TV presenters and is renowned for her skills in mathematics. She has a degree in engineering from the University of Cambridge. Carol has a keen interest in coding and feels strongly that every child should have the chance to learn such a valuable skill. She has hosted numerous TV shows on science and technology, such as *Tomorrow's World* and *How 2*, on the BBC, ITV, and Channel 4. Whether co-hosting Channel 4's *Countdown* for 26 years, becoming the second-best-selling female non-fiction author of the noughties in the UK, or advising Prime Minister David Cameron on mathematics education in British schools, Carol has a passion and devotion to explaining mathematics, science, and technology in an exciting and easily understandable way.

DR JON WOODCOCK MA (OXON) has a degree in physics from the University of Oxford and a PhD in computational astrophysics from the University of London. He started coding at the age of eight and has programmed all kinds of computers, from single-chip microcontrollers to world-class supercomputers. His many projects include giant space simulations, research in high-tech companies, and intelligent robots made from junk. Jon has a passion for science and technology education, giving talks on space and running computer programming clubs in schools. He has worked on numerous science and technology books as a contributor and consultant, including DK's *Computer Coding for Kids* and *Computer Coding Made Easy*.

Contents

Find out more at:
www.dk.com/computercoding

Foreword

Many of the people who shaped our digital world started out by coding games for fun. Bill Gates, cofounder of Microsoft, wrote his first computer program at the age of 13 – a noughts and crosses game. Just a few years later a teenage Steve Jobs and his friend Steve Wozniak, who later founded Apple together, created the arcade game Breakout.

They started coding simply because they enjoyed it. They had no idea how far it would take them or that the companies they were to build would change the world. You might be the next one like them. Coding doesn't have to become a career, but it's an amazing skill and can unlock exciting doors to your future. Or you might just want to play around with code for the fun of it.

Computer games open up worlds of imagination. They reach out across the internet and allow us to play together. They are packed with creativity, from music, stories, and art to ingenious coding. And we're hooked on them: so much so that the games industry is now worth more than the movie industry. It's huge.

And now, instead of being just a player, you can become a game maker too. You can take control of every aspect of those imaginary worlds: how they look, sound, and feel. You get to invent the stories, the heroes, the villains, and the landscapes.

But first you need to take control of your computer. To tell a computer what to do, you need to speak its language and become a programmer! Thanks to languages like Scratch™, it's never been easier. Just follow the simple steps in this book to build each game and you'll see what goes on inside each one. Follow the chapters in order, and you'll pick up the essential skills you need to design and build your very own games.

Carol Vorderman

CAROL VORDERMAN

Let's get coding!

Computer games

What makes a good game?

Some games have a magical quality that makes you want to play them time and again. Game designers call it playability. To make a game with great playability, you need to think about all the ingredients that make up the game and how they mix together.

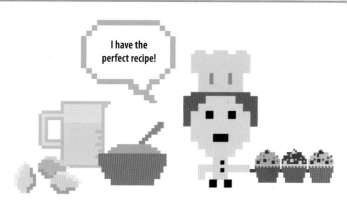

I have the perfect recipe!

◁ **Characters**

In most games, the player uses an on-screen character to enter the game world. It could an animal, a princess, a race car, or even just a simple bubble. To create a sense of danger or competition, such games usually also have enemy characters that the player has to defeat or escape from.

△ **Mechanics**

These are the "verbs" in a game – actions such as running, jumping, flying, capturing objects, casting spells, and using weapons. The mechanics are the core of the game, and well-designed mechanics make a good game.

△ **Objects**

Nearly all games include objects, from stars and coins that boost health or scores to keys that unlock doors. Not all objects are good – some get in the player's way, sap their health, or steal their treasures. Objects can also work together to create puzzles for the player to solve.

◁ **Rules**

The rules in a game tell you what you're allowed and not allowed to do. For example, can you walk through walls or do they block your path? Can you stop and think or do you have to beat the clock?

△ Goals

Every game challenges the player to achieve some kind of goal, whether it's winning a race, conquering an enemy, beating a high score, or simply surviving for as long you can. Most games have lots of small goals, such as unlocking doors to new levels or winning new vehicles or skills.

◁ **World**

Think about the world in which a game is played. Is it 2D or 3D? Does the player view the game from above, from the side, or from within? Does the game world have walls or boundaries that limit the player's movement or is it open like the outdoors?

◁ **Controls**

Keyboards, mice, joysticks, and motion sensors all make good controllers. Games are more fun when the player feels in complete control of their character, so the controls should be easy to master and the computer should respond instantly.

△ Difficulty level

A game's no fun if it's too easy or hard. Many games make the challenges easy at the start, while the player is learning, and more difficult later as their skills improve. Getting the difficulty level just right is the key to making a great game.

■ ■ **GAME DESIGN**

Playability

Games don't have to be complicated to make people want to play them over and over again. One of the first successful computer games was a simple tennis simulator called Pong. The ball was a white square and the racquets were white lines that could only move up and down. Although there were no fancy graphics, people loved Pong because it had great playability. They could compete against friends, just like in real tennis, and it was just hard enough to demand intense concentration and a steady hand, leaving players always wanting another game.

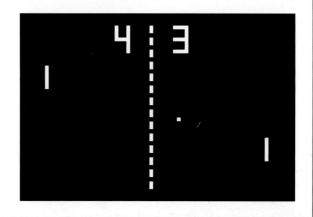

Atmosphere

A good game, just like a film or a book, can draw you in and change the way you feel by creating a certain atmosphere. Here are some of the tricks game designers use to conjure up an atmosphere.

◁ Telling stories

A background story helps set the scene for a game and gives meaning to the player's actions. Blockbuster games have movie-like plots with twists, but even simple games can benefit from some kind of story if it makes players feel like they're on a mission. Thinking of a story also helps you give a game a consistent theme.

△ Boo!

Do things jump out at the player? Fear and suspense can make a game scary and put the player on edge. What's around the next corner? What's behind that door? The wait can be worse than the scare!

▷ Sound

Sounds can have a strong effect on how we feel. Changing the tune can make the same scene feel exciting, scary, or even silly, and a sudden noise after a quiet spell can cause a jolt of terror. Modern games use realistic sound effects to make players feel like they're inside the action.

▷ Faster, faster!

The speed of a game changes the level of excitement a player feels. It's easy to stay calm when you can stop and think about what to do next, but with a ticking clock and fast music, you can't help but feel under pressure.

◁ Colour scheme

You can change the atmosphere in a game simply by altering the colours. Bright blue, yellow, and green feels warm and sunny, for instance, while icy blues and white feel wintry, and darker colours make a game feel spooky.

▽ **Graphics**

The graphics in the first games were simple geometric shapes, but as computers became more powerful, the graphics in games got better. Many console games now feature photorealistic 3D images, but games based on simple, cartoon-like graphics are as popular as ever and can help create a more playful atmosphere.

▪▪ GAME DESIGN

Virtual reality

Virtual reality goggles could make the games of the future much more realistic. They work by presenting each eye with a slightly different image, creating a 3D experience. Motion sensors in the headset track the player's movements and adjust the images to match, allowing the player to turn around and look in any direction, just like in the real world. As a result, the player feels like they are inside the game world rather than watching it through a screen.

Where are you?

One of the easiest ways to create atmosphere is to give a game a location by adding a background image. To make the illusion more convincing, make sure the game's characters match the setting – don't put race cars in the deep sea or unicorns in outer space, for instance.

◁ **Snow and ice**
A snowy scene is the backdrop for a race along an icy road.

△ **Spooky forest**
A dark forest is the perfect setting for ghosts, ghouls, and witches.

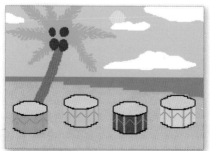

△ **Tropical beach**
A sunny beach creates a carnival mood for the colourful steel drums.

△ **Deep sea adventure**
Octopuses and starfish fit well with this underwater scene.

Types of game

Games come in all shapes and sizes, but most fit into one of just a few main categories, called genres. Some gamers like the platform games genre best, whereas others prefer racing games or strategy games. What are your favourite genres?

◁ **Traditional**
When you can't find an opponent to play, a computer can challenge you to a game of cards, chess, or a million other popular board games.

△ **Role-playing**
Dungeons, dragons, and castles feature in these adventure games. Players may roam freely or follow a set storyline, with their character developing specialist skills as it advances, such as casting spells or sword fighting. Some role-playing games are played online, allowing lots of players to interact in the same game world.

▷ **Racing**
Racing games create the illusion of speed by making the scenery scroll past the player's viewpoint. To succeed, you need to learn each racetrack inside out so you can start tricky manoevres in advance.

△ **Sandbox**
Some games force players along a set path, but sandbox games are the opposite: they give you complete freedom to explore the game world at your own pace and choose different quests within it.

△ **Combat**
Nimble fingerwork is vital for games involving close-quarters combat. The key to success is knowing when and how to use many different attack and defence moves, from slams and somersaults to special powers.

▷ Strategy

Decisions, decisions. What are the best choices to make if you're running a zoo, fighting a war, or building a whole civilization? Strategy games give the player godlike powers over many different characters at once, but you have to manage resources cleverly or your empire will collapse.

△ Simulator

If you want a puppy but don't want the bother of feeding and walking it, a virtual pet might suit you. Simulators aim to re-create real-life situations. Some are more than just a game: flight simulators are so accurate and realistic that professional pilots use them for training.

◁ Music and dance

Dance-mat games involve tapping the feet or jumping over a stream of obstacles in time to the rhythm. Music games allow you to play along with a virtual band using a pretend instrument. You need to hit the right notes on time to complete each level.

△ Sport

Play the game of your choice as your favourite team, set in a realistic stadium with roaring crowds. Sports games let you compete in famous tournaments such as the football World Cup, with the computer referee ensuring fair play.

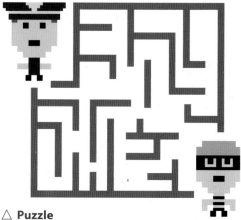

△ Puzzle

Some people love to exercise their brains with puzzles. There are many different types, from colourful tile-matching games to number puzzles and escape games, in which you need to use your imagination to find your way from room to room.

How coding works

A computer can't think for itself – it works by blindly following instructions. It can only carry out a complex task if that task has been broken down into simple steps that tell it exactly what to do and in what order. Writing these instructions in a language a computer understands is called coding.

Planning a game

Imagine you want to create a game in which you fly a parrot over a river, collecting apples as they drift downstream but avoiding an angry lion. You would need to give the computer a separate set of instructions for each object in the game: the apple, the parrot, and the lion.

The player makes the parrot fly left and right with the left and right arrow keys.

Pressing the space key makes the parrot dive, but the game ends if you touch the lion.

Score 10

The player wins a point each time the parrot gets an apple.

The apple drifts downstream over and over. It reappears on the left if the parrot takes it.

The lion walks left and right, following the parrot.

▽ **Apple**

You can't simply tell the computer that the apple drifts down the river and vanishes when the parrot eats it. Instead, you need to break down this complicated task into a set of very simple steps as shown here.

Jump to the left edge of the screen.

Repeat the following steps over and over again:

Move a bit to the right.

If I get to the right edge of the screen then

jump back to the left edge.

If I touch the parrot then

add one to the parrot's score and

jump back to the left edge.

▷ **Parrot**

The parrot is more complicated than the apple because the player controls it and it can move up, down, left, and right. Even so, it's possible to make all this work by writing a sequence of simple instructions.

Jump to the top right of the screen.

Repeat these steps in turn:

> If the player presses the left arrow then

>> move a bit to the left if I can.

> If the player presses the right arrow then

>> move a bit to the right if I can.

> If the player presses the space key then

>> move all the way to the bottom of the screen taking a second and

>> move all the way back to the top taking a second

▷ **Lion**

The lion is the player's enemy and can end the game if the parrot touches it. It is controlled by a simple program.

Jump to the middle of the screen.

Repeat these steps in turn:

> If the parrot is to my left then

>> move a bit to my left.

> If the parrot is to my right then

>> move a bit to my right.

> If the parrot touches me then

>> stop the game.

· · LINGO

Programming languages

The instructions on this page are in simple English, but if you wanted to create the game on a computer, you would need to translate them into special words that the computer can understand: a programming language. Writing programs with a programming language is called coding or programming. This book uses the programming language Scratch, which is ideal for learning about coding and great for making games.

Getting started

Introducing Scratch

All the games in this book are made with a programming language called Scratch. Scratch is easy to learn because you don't have to type any complicated code. Instead, you build programs from ready-made blocks.

The characters and other objects in Scratch games are called sprites.

Starting from scratch

A project in Scratch usually starts with choosing what objects, or sprites, will appear in the game. Scratch has a large library of ready-made sprites to get you started.

Sprites

Sprites are the things that move about or react in the game. They can be anything from animals and people to pizzas or spaceships. You can bring each sprite to life on screen with a list of instructions called a script.

The cat sprite appears whenever you start a new Scratch project.

Scripts

Scripts are made of blocks that you can drag with a computer mouse and join together like jigsaw pieces. Each block contains one instruction so it's easy to understand.

Hello!

```
when  space ▼  key pressed
move ( 20 ) steps
say    Hello!
```

Working together

Games are usually made up of several sprites working together, each controlled by their own script. Scripts make sprites move about, crash into each other, create sounds, and change colour or shape.

Some sprites act as enemies to make a game more difficult.

HELP!

EXPERT TIPS

Experimenting

Scratch is all about experimenting. Once you've built a game, it's easy to add things to it or change how it works by tinkering with the script. You can see the effect of your changes straight away.

A typical Scratch project

Once you've built a script, you can click the green flag to see what it does. All the action takes place in a part of the Scratch window called the "stage". Sprites move about on the stage, often in front of a background image that helps create atmosphere.

The red button stops a program.

The green flag starts, or runs, the program.

▷ **Running a program**
Starting, or "running", a program activates the scripts that you've built. To make the stage fill your whole computer screen, click the blue symbol in the top left.

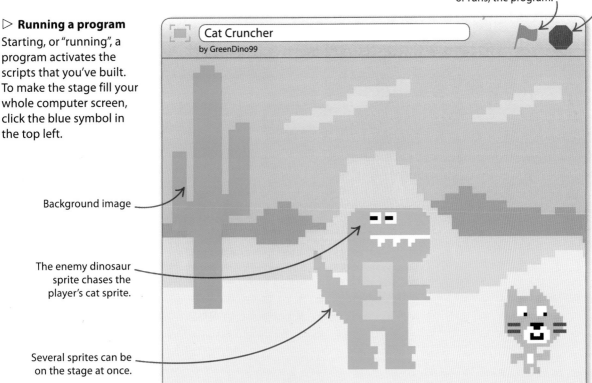

Cat Cruncher
by GreenDino99

Background image

The enemy dinosaur sprite chases the player's cat sprite.

Several sprites can be on the stage at once.

▽ **Making sprites move**
In a typical game, the player moves one sprite and the other sprites are programmed to move automatically. The script below makes the dinosaur in this project chase the cat.

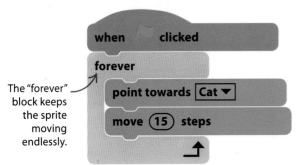

when clicked

forever

The "forever" block keeps the sprite moving endlessly.

point towards Cat ▼

move 15 steps

Getting Scratch

In order to try the projects in this book, you'll need to set up Scratch on a desktop or laptop computer. The two ways of setting up Scratch (online and offline) are shown below.

LINGO

Why "Scratch"?

Scratch is named after "scratching", a technique rappers and DJs use to remix music on a turntable. The Scratch programming language lets you copy other people's projects and remix them to make your own unique versions.

Online Scratch

If you have a reliable internet connection, you can run Scratch online in a browser window without downloading anything. You will need to set up a Scratch account.

1 Join Scratch

To set up the online version, visit the Scratch website at **scratch.mit.edu** and click "Join Scratch". You will need to set up an account with a username and password. Your games will stay private unless you click "Share", which will publish them on the web.

2 Sign in

After you've joined the Scratch website, click "Sign in" and enter your username and password. It's best not to use your real name as your username. Click "Create" at the top of the screen to start a new project. If you use the online version of Scratch, you can access your projects from any computer.

Offline Scratch

You can also download the Scratch program to your computer so you can use it offline. This is particularly useful if your internet connection is unreliable.

1 Install Scratch

For the offline version of Scratch, go to **scratch.mit.edu/scratch2download**. Follow the instructions on screen to download the installation files, then double-click them. After installation, a Scratch icon will appear on your desktop.

2 Launch Scratch

Double-click the icon on the desktop and Scratch will open, ready for you to begin programming. There's no need to create a user account if you use the offline version of Scratch.

△ **Operating system**

The online version of Scratch works well on Windows, Ubuntu, and Mac computers, though it won't work on tablets. The offline version of Scratch works well on Windows and Mac computers. If your computer uses Ubuntu, try the online version instead.

△ **Hardware**

You can use Scratch on desktop or laptop computers, but it's easier if you use a mouse rather than a touchpad. Scratch apps for tablets and smartphones are also being developed.

◁ **Saving**

If you use Scratch offline, remember to save from time to time. The online version saves automatically. Online, you can undo all the changes you've made since you last opened a project by choosing "Revert" in the File menu.

Old and new versions

This book is based on Scratch 2.0, the latest version at the time of writing. The projects in this book will not work with older versions of Scratch, so make sure you have 2.0.

▽ **Version 1.4**

In older versions of Scratch, such as Scratch 1.4, the stage is on the right and the scripts area is in the middle.

▷ **Version 2.0**

This version of Scratch was released in 2013. New features include a "Backpack" for storing costumes, media, and scripts; a cloning function; a sound editor; and a more sophisticated paint editor.

Scratch tour

The Scratch window is divided into several different areas. Scripts are built on the right, while the stage on the left shows the game running.

Switch to full screen view

Change language

Menus

Cursor tools

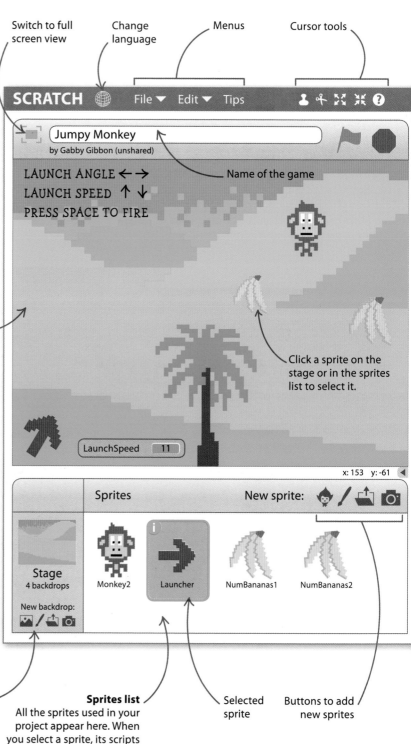

Name of the game

Click a sprite on the stage or in the sprites list to select it.

The stage
When you play a game or run any other kind of project in Scratch, you see the action happening on the stage, which serves as a miniature screen. You can see changes to your script take effect immediately on the stage simply by clicking the green flag button to run the project.

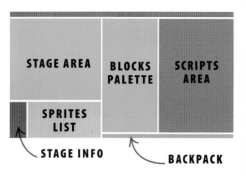

STAGE AREA	BLOCKS PALETTE	SCRIPTS AREA
SPRITES LIST		
STAGE INFO	BACKPACK	

△ **Scratch window**
The stage and sprites list occupy the left of the Scratch window, while script-building areas are on the right. The tabs above the scripts area reveal other Scratch features.

Click these icons to change the backdrop image on the stage.

Sprites list
All the sprites used in your project appear here. When you select a sprite, its scripts appear in the scripts area.

Selected sprite

Buttons to add new sprites

Keep the Scripts tab selected to build scripts.

The Costumes tab lets you change how sprites look.

Use the Sounds tab to add music and sound effects to games.

Scripts area
You can drag blocks into this part of the Scratch window and join them together to build scripts for each sprite in your game.

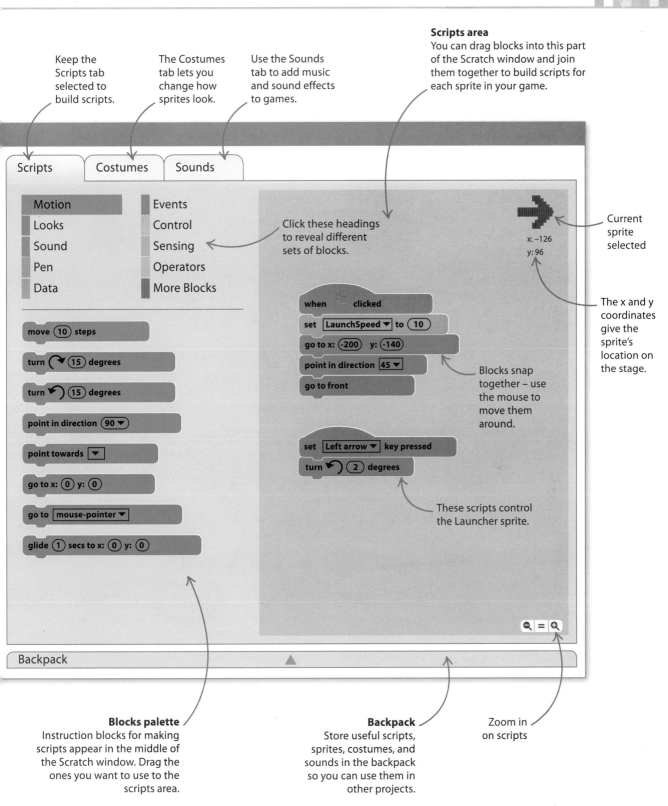

Scripts   Costumes   Sounds

Motion
Looks
Sound
Pen
Data

Events
Control
Sensing
Operators
More Blocks

Click these headings to reveal different sets of blocks.

Current sprite selected

x: −126
y: 96

move (10) steps

turn ↻ (15) degrees

turn ↺ (15) degrees

point in direction (90 ▼)

point towards [▼]

go to x: (0) y: (0)

go to mouse-pointer ▼

glide (1) secs to x: (0) y: (0)

when clicked
set LaunchSpeed ▼ to (10)
go to x: (-200) y: (-140)
point in direction 45 ▼
go to front

Blocks snap together – use the mouse to move them around.

The x and y coordinates give the sprite's location on the stage.

set Left arrow ▼ key pressed
turn ↺ (2) degrees

These scripts control the Launcher sprite.

Q = Q

Backpack

Blocks palette
Instruction blocks for making scripts appear in the middle of the Scratch window. Drag the ones you want to use to the scripts area.

Backpack
Store useful scripts, sprites, costumes, and sounds in the backpack so you can use them in other projects.

Zoom in on scripts

Star
Hunter

How to build Star Hunter

Welcome to your first Scratch game: Star Hunter, a fast-paced, underwater treasure hunt. Just follow the simple steps in this chapter to build the game, and then challenge a friend to beat your score.

AIM OF THE GAME

The aim of this game is to collect as many golden stars as you can. Use the cat to collect the stars, but watch out for deadly octopuses. You'll need to move quickly to succeed. The main sprites in the game are shown below.

◁ **Cat**
Move the cat around the screen with your computer mouse – the cat sprite follows the mouse-pointer.

◁ **Octopuses**
The octopuses patrol the seas but they swim more slowly than you. If you touch one, it's game over!

◁ **Stars**
These appear one at a time in random places. Touch a star to score a point.

Click this icon to make the game fill your screen.

Type in the name of your game.

The score shows how many stars you've collected.

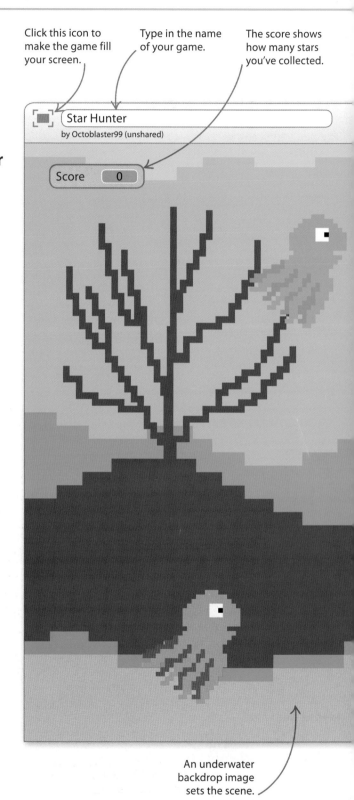

Star Hunter
by Octoblaster99 (unshared)

Score   0

An underwater backdrop image sets the scene.

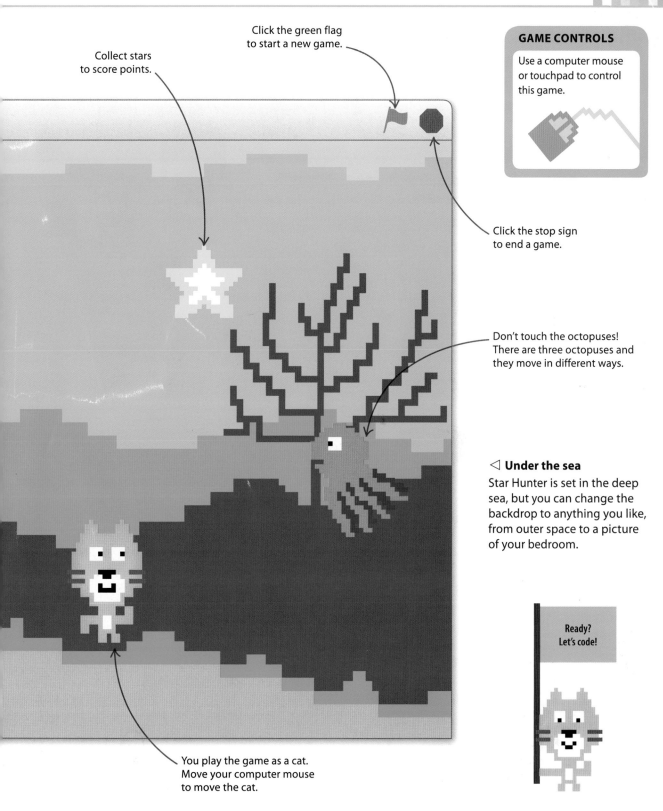

Click the green flag
to start a new game.

Collect stars
to score points.

GAME CONTROLS

Use a computer mouse
or touchpad to control
this game.

Click the stop sign
to end a game.

Don't touch the octopuses!
There are three octopuses and
they move in different ways.

◁ **Under the sea**
Star Hunter is set in the deep
sea, but you can change the
backdrop to anything you like,
from outer space to a picture
of your bedroom.

Ready?
Let's code!

You play the game as a cat.
Move your computer mouse
to move the cat.

Building scripts

Like any Scratch program, Star Hunter is made by joining together coloured blocks like jigsaw pieces. Each block is an instruction that tells a sprite what to do. Let's start by programming the game's main sprite: the cat.

1 Start Scratch and choose either "create" or "New Project". You'll see a screen like the one below, with the cat sprite in place. In the middle is a set of blue instruction blocks.

Clicking the buttons here reveals different sets of blocks.

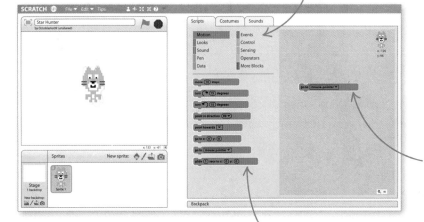

Drag your chosen blocks here to build a script.

Choose blocks from the list in the middle.

2 We'll program the cat to move wherever the player moves the computer mouse. Click on the "go to mouse-pointer" block and drag it to the right part of the screen – the scripts area.

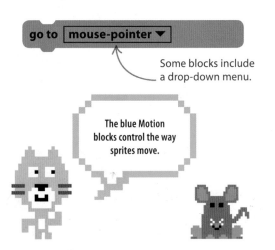

`go to | mouse-pointer ▼`

Some blocks include a drop-down menu.

> The blue Motion blocks control the way sprites move.

3 Now select the yellow Control button and look for a "forever" block.

Scripts	Costumes	Sounds

Motion	Events
Looks	Control
Sound	Sensing
Pen	Operators
Data	More Blocks

Click Control to reveal the yellow blocks.

`wait (10) secs`

`repeat (10)`

`forever`

Drag the "forever" block to the scripts area.

4 Drag it to the right and drop it over the blue block. It will wrap around it like this:

forever
    go to [mouse-pointer ▼]

5 Next, select the brown Events button. Look for a block with a green flag. Drag it to the right and add it to the top of your script. Read through the script and think about what each block does.

when ⚑ clicked
forever
    go to [mouse-pointer ▼]

This block starts the game when you click the green flag.

This block makes the cat move with the player's mouse-pointer.

This block makes the block inside it repeat over and over again.

6 Now look at the top right of the stage – you'll see a green flag. Click this to run your script.

Click the green flag to play.

You can stop the script by clicking the red stop button.

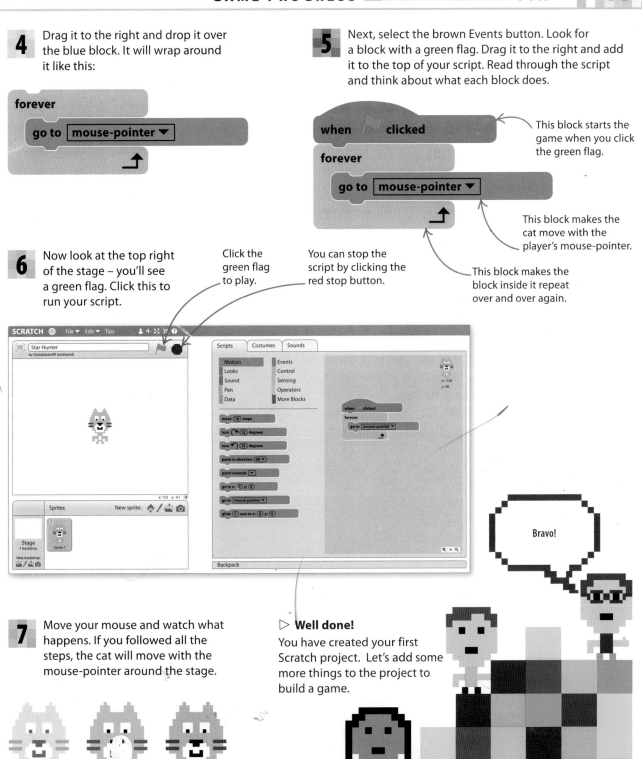

7 Move your mouse and watch what happens. If you followed all the steps, the cat will move with the mouse-pointer around the stage.

▷ **Well done!**
You have created your first Scratch project. Let's add some more things to the project to build a game.

Bravo!

8 The poor cat is called "Sprite1". Let's fix that. In the sprites list, select Sprite1 (the cat) and click on the blue "i" in the corner to get more information about the sprite. Change the name to "Cat".

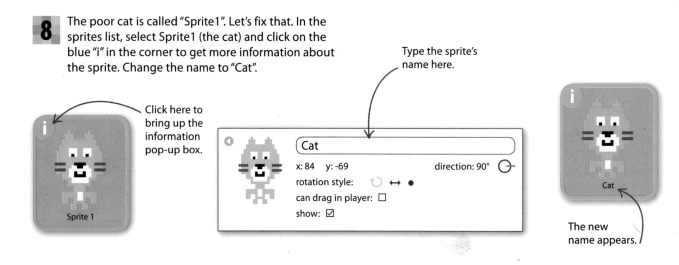

Click here to bring up the information pop-up box.

Sprite 1

Type the sprite's name here.

Cat

x: 84   y: -69   direction: 90°
rotation style:
can drag in player: ☐
show: ☑

Cat

The new name appears.

Setting the scene

At the moment the stage is just a boring white rectangle. Let's create some atmosphere by adding scenery and sound effects. To change the scenery, we add a "backdrop" image.

9 To the left of the sprites list is a button to add a picture from the backdrop library. Click it and look for "underwater2". Select the image and click "OK". The backdrop will now fill the stage.

The backdrop is just decoration and doesn't affect the sprites.

Star Hunter
by Octoblaster99 (unshared)

Stage
1 backdrop

New backdrop:

Click this icon to open the backdrop library.

Sound effects

Now we'll add a bubbling sound to the cat sprite to make it sound like we're underwater.

10 Highlight the cat in the sprites list and then click the Sounds tab above the blocks palette. Click the speaker icon to choose a sound from the library.

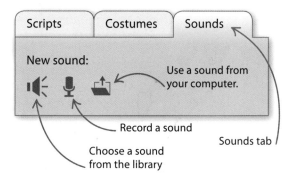

Scripts | Costumes | Sounds

New sound:

Use a sound from your computer.

Record a sound

Sounds tab

Choose a sound from the library

11 Look for "bubbles" in the library. You can preview sounds by clicking the play symbol. To load a sound into the game, click the speaker icon and then "OK". Now you'll see bubbles in your list of sounds.

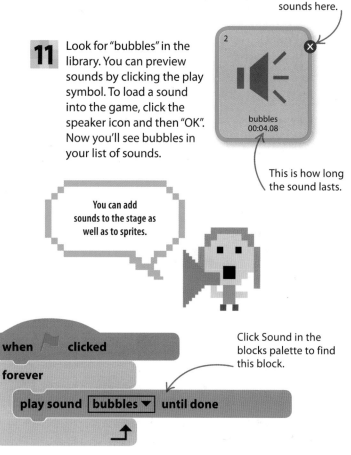

Delete sounds here.

bubbles
00:04.08

This is how long the sound lasts.

> You can add sounds to the stage as well as to sprites.

12 Click the Scripts tab and add the following script to the cat sprite, but leave the old script in place as you need both. The new script repeats the bubbles sound. The "play sound ... done" block waits for the sound to finish before letting it start again. Run the game to hear the sound effect.

when ⚑ clicked

forever

play sound bubbles ▼ until done

Click Sound in the blocks palette to find this block.

. . . **EXPERT TIPS**

Loops

A loop is a section of code that repeats over and over again. The "forever" block creates a loop that carries on forever, but other types of loop can repeat an action a fixed number of times. Loops are very common in almost all computer programming languages.

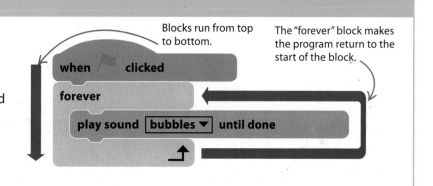

Blocks run from top to bottom.

The "forever" block makes the program return to the start of the block.

when ⚑ clicked

forever

play sound bubbles ▼ until done

Add an enemy

The game needs an enemy to make things more interesting. Let's add an octopus with a deadly sting. The octopus will patrol the stage, moving left and right, and the player will have to keep out of its way or it's game over.

13 To add a second sprite to the project, click the icon shown below to open up the sprite library. Choose the octopus and click "OK".

Click here to open the sprite library.

The octopus sprite will appear in your sprites list.

Octopus

14 Add the following script to the octopus sprite. To find the blue blocks, click on Motion in the blocks palette. The two Motion blocks used here make the octopus move left and right across the stage.

This block runs the script when the game begins.

Motion blocks are dark blue and control the way sprites move.

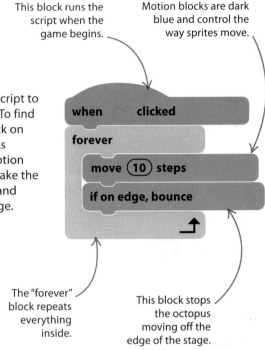

The "forever" block repeats everything inside.

This block stops the octopus moving off the edge of the stage.

15 Now run the script. The octopus will patrol left and right, but you'll notice it's upside down half the time. We can fix this by changing the way the sprite turns around when it changes direction. Highlight the octopus and click the blue "i". In the pop-up box, there are three options after "rotation style".

16 Choose the middle option and run the project. The octopus should now stay the right way up and facing forwards all the time. You can adjust its starting position on the screen by dragging it with the mouse.

The middle option makes the sprite flip sideways when it bounces.

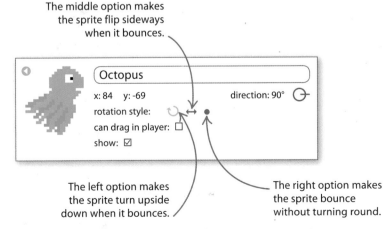

The left option makes the sprite turn upside down when it bounces.

The right option makes the sprite bounce without turning round.

Collisions

So far the octopus and cat move through each other without anything happening. We need to add a script to make them stop moving when they collide. Collision detection is very important in computer games.

17 Highlight the octopus and drag a yellow "if then" block to an empty part of the scripts area. Now add a pale blue "touching" block to the top of the "if then" block. Click the drop-down menu and choose "Cat". This script will help the octopus detect the cat.

Sensing blocks are pale blue.

This block detects a collision.

18 Choose Control in the blocks palette again, and add a "stop all" block to the middle of the "if then" block. This will stop all action if the octopus is touching the cat, ending the game.

This block ends the game when the sprites collide.

19 Now add the "if then" blocks you've built to the octopus's main script, placing it carefully after the blue Motion blocks. Also, add a "wait 0.5 sec" before the loop. Run the project and see what happens.

The "wait" block adds a slight delay before the octopus starts moving.

The "stop all" block only runs if the answer to the question in the "touching" block is yes.

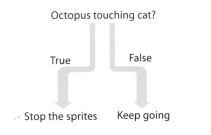

"if then"

You make decisions every day. If it's raining, you might use an umbrella. If it isn't, you don't. Computer programs do the same thing by using what programmers call conditional statements, such as "if then". When Scratch reaches an "if then" block, it runs the blocks inside only if the statement is true.

Octopus touching cat?

True | False

Stop the sprites | Keep going

More enemies

Let's add more enemies to the game, but to make things more challenging, we'll set them moving in different directions. We can tell each sprite exactly which way to go by using a block that works like a compass.

20 Add a purple "set size" block to the top of the octopus's script, after the "when clicked" block. Set the octopus's size to 35% to make the game a bit easier. Then add a blue "point in direction" block.

21 To change the octopus's direction, click on the window in the "point in direction" block and type 135 in place of 90. This will make the octopus move diagonally.

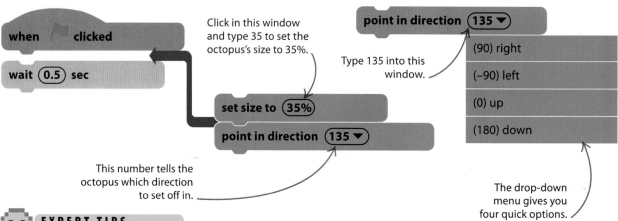

Click in this window and type 35 to set the octopus's size to 35%.

Type 135 into this window.

This number tells the octopus which direction to set off in.

(90) right

(−90) left

(0) up

(180) down

The drop-down menu gives you four quick options.

Directions

Scratch uses degrees to set direction. You can choose any number from −179° to 180°. Negative numbers point sprites left; positive numbers point them right. Use 0° to go up and 180° to go straight down.

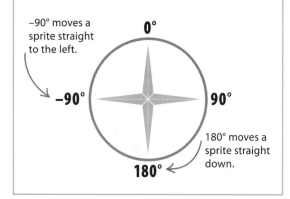

−90° moves a sprite straight to the left.

0°

−90°

90°

180°

180° moves a sprite straight down.

22 Now we can duplicate our octopus to create more enemies. Right-click on the octopus in the sprites list (or control-click if you have a Mac) and choose "duplicate". Copies of the Octopus sprite will appear in the sprites list, named Octopus2 and Octopus3. Each will have a copy of the first octopus's script.

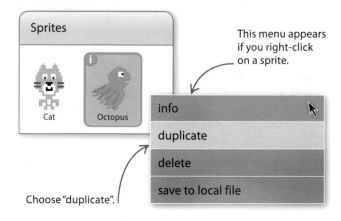

Sprites

Cat

Octopus

This menu appears if you right-click on a sprite.

info

duplicate

delete

save to local file

Choose "duplicate".

23 To make the octopuses move in different directions, change the number in the "point in direction" block for each new octopus. Leave the first Octopus sprite's direction as 135, but set Octopus2 to 0 and Octopus3 to 90. Run the project and try to avoid all the enemies.

24 If it's too hard to stay alive, make the octopuses slower by lowering the number of steps in their "move" blocks to two. Remember to change the script for all three octopus sprites.

Changing this number adjusts the octopus's speed.

```
move (2) steps
if on edge, bounce
```

25 For more variety, let's make one of the octopuses set off in a random direction. To do this, we use a green "pick random" block. This is Scratch's way of rolling a dice to generate a random number. Choose Operators in the blocks palette to find the block and add it to the first octopus's script. Run the project a few times to see the octopus choose different starting directions.

Type –179 in the first window.

Type 180 in the second window.

```
when        clicked
set size to (35%)
point in direction    pick random (–179) to (180)
wait (0.5) sec
forever
    move (2) steps
    if on edge, bounce
    if        touching [Cat ▼] ?        then
        stop [all ▼]
```

EXPERT TIPS
Random numbers

Why do so many games use dice? Dice create surprises in a game because they make different things happen to each player. A random number is one you can't predict in advance, just like the roll of a dice. You can get the cat to say a random dice roll using this simple code.

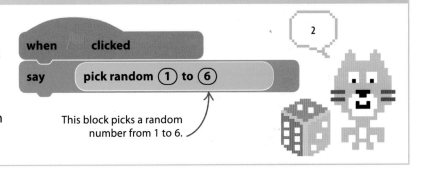

```
when        clicked
say        pick random (1) to (6)
```

This block picks a random number from 1 to 6.

Collecting stars

In many games, the player has to collect valuable items to win points or to stay alive. In Star Hunter, we use golden stars as underwater treasure that the player has to collect. We'll use random numbers again to make each star appear in a new place.

26 Click the "choose new sprite" symbol ✿ in the sprites list and choose the "Star1" sprite from the library.

Star1

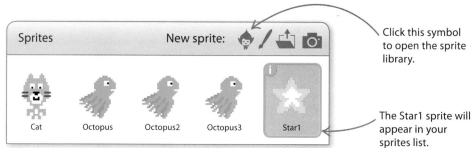

Click this symbol to open the sprite library.

The Star1 sprite will appear in your sprites list.

27 Add the following script to Star1. This script will make the star move to a random new location whenever the cat touches it. The green blocks create random numbers called coordinates, which Scratch uses to pinpoint locations on the stage.

The "if then" block checks whether the cat is touching the star.

The "go to" block only runs if the answer to the question is yes.

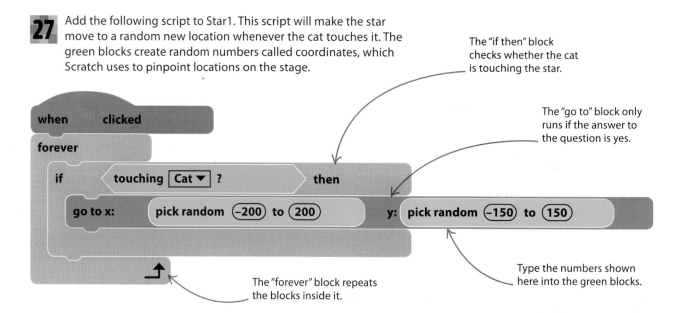

The "forever" block repeats the blocks inside it.

Type the numbers shown here into the green blocks.

28 To see the star's coordinates change when it moves, choose Motion in the blocks palette and put ticks by "x position" and "y position". Now run the game: you'll see the star's x and y coordinates update each time the cat makes it move. Untick both boxes before you carry on.

Star1: x position `60`

Star1: y position `78`

Using coordinates

To pinpoint a location on the stage, Scratch uses numbers called coordinates. These work just like graph coordinates, with x numbers for horizontal positions and y numbers for vertical. To find the coordinates for a spot on the stage, just count the steps across and up from the centre of the stage. Positive coordinates are up or right, negative coordinates are down or left. Every spot on the stage has a unique pair of coordinates that can be used to send a sprite to that position.

The x axis is bigger than the y axis and extends from –240 to 240.

29 You can add a sound effect that plays when the cat touches a star. First make sure the star is selected in the sprites list, then click the Sounds tab above the blocks palette. Click the speaker symbol 🔊 to open the sound library. Choose "fairydust" and click "OK". Now add the pink "play sound" block to the star's script and choose "fairydust" in the drop-down list.

Insert the "play sound" block into Star1's existing script, then use the drop-down menu to choose which sound to play.

```
if        touching  Cat ▼  ?           then
    play sound  fairydust ▼
    go to x:    pick random (-200) to (200)    y:  pick random (-150) to (150)
```

Keeping score

Computer games often need to keep track of vital statistics such as the player's score or health. We call these changing numbers "variables". To keep track of the player's score in Star Hunter, we'll create a variable that counts the number of stars the player has collected.

30 With any sprite selected, choose Data in the blocks palette. Click on the button "Make a Variable".

Click here to create a new variable.

31 A pop-up box appears asking you to give your variable a name. Type "Score" in the box. Make sure the option "For all sprites" is selected and hit "OK".

This option makes the variable available for every sprite.

32 You'll see a set of new blocks appear, including one for the score. Make sure the box next to it is ticked to make the score appear on the stage.

33 The score counter will appear in the top left of the stage but you can drag it anywhere you like.

You can use the mouse to move the score display.

34 We want the score to start at zero and increase by one each time the cat touches a star. Select the star sprite and add the two orange Data blocks below to its script.

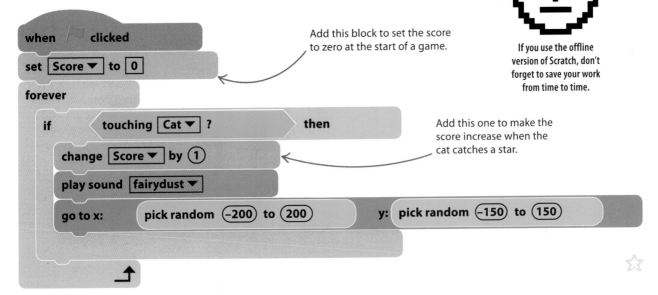

Add this block to set the score to zero at the start of a game.

Add this one to make the score increase when the cat catches a star.

If you use the offline version of Scratch, don't forget to save your work from time to time.

35 Now click the green flag to run the script and see what happens when the cat collects each star. See if you can collect 20 stars without bumping into an octopus.

EXPERT TIPS

Variables

A variable works like a box that you can store information in, such as a number than can change. In maths, we use letters for variables, such as x and y. In computer programming, we give variables names such as "Score" and use them for storing not just numbers but any kind of information. Try to choose a name that tells you what the variable is for, such as "Speed" or "Score". Most computer languages won't let you put spaces in the names of variables, so a good tip is to combine words. Instead of using "dog speed", for instance, type "DogSpeed".

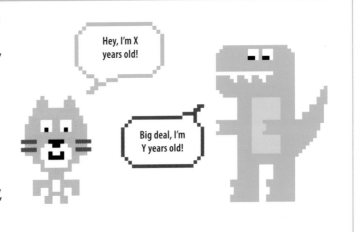

Hey, I'm X years old!

Big deal, I'm Y years old!

Better enemies

Now we have a working game, we can test it and experiment with changes that make it easier, harder, or – most important – more fun. One way to make the game more interesting is to make the three octopuses do different things.

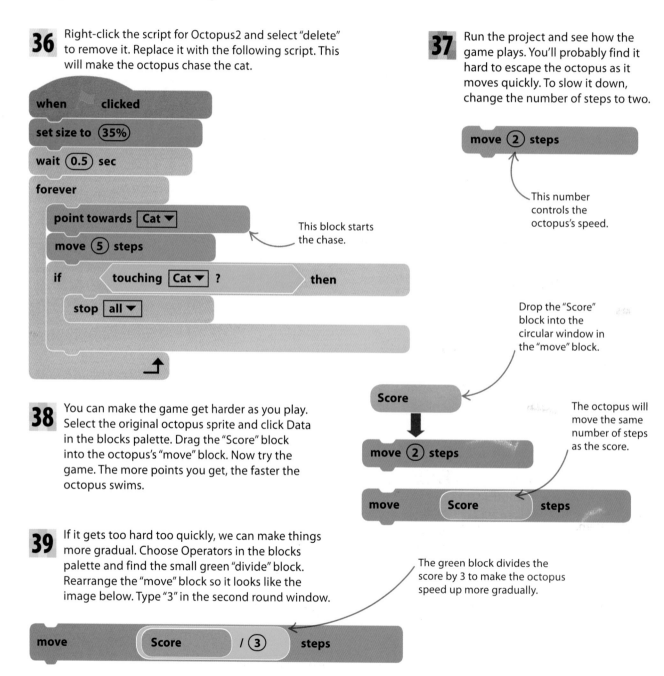

36 Right-click the script for Octopus2 and select "delete" to remove it. Replace it with the following script. This will make the octopus chase the cat.

when [ ] clicked
set size to (35%)
wait (0.5) sec
forever
  point towards [Cat ▼]
  move (5) steps
  if < touching [Cat ▼] ? > then
    stop [all ▼]

This block starts the chase.

37 Run the project and see how the game plays. You'll probably find it hard to escape the octopus as it moves quickly. To slow it down, change the number of steps to two.

move (2) steps

This number controls the octopus's speed.

Drop the "Score" block into the circular window in the "move" block.

Score

move (2) steps

move (Score) steps

The octopus will move the same number of steps as the score.

38 You can make the game get harder as you play. Select the original octopus sprite and click Data in the blocks palette. Drag the "Score" block into the octopus's "move" block. Now try the game. The more points you get, the faster the octopus swims.

39 If it gets too hard too quickly, we can make things more gradual. Choose Operators in the blocks palette and find the small green "divide" block. Rearrange the "move" block so it looks like the image below. Type "3" in the second round window.

The green block divides the score by 3 to make the octopus speed up more gradually.

move (Score / (3)) steps

40 Now we'll make Octopus3 patrol in a regular pattern. To do this, we'll use a new Motion block that makes it glide smoothly from point to point, rather than moving in steps. Replace the script for Octopus3 with the following two scripts. These run at the same time, one checking for collisions and the other moving the octopus around its patrol route.

The two scripts are separate in the scripts area.

Type these numbers into the "glide" blocks.

41 Now run the project and watch Octopus3. It should swim in a repeating triangle pattern.

To change the shape of the triangle, try different numbers in the "glide" blocks.

I feel like I'm swimming in circles...

Hacks and tweaks

You've built a fun game, but that's just the beginning. Scratch makes it easy to change and adapt games as much as you want. You might find bugs that need fixing, or you might want to make the game harder or easier. Here are some suggestions to get you started.

▽ **Debug Octopus2**

If Octopus2 ends up in the top-right corner at the end of a game, it can trap the player in the next game and end it too quickly. This is a bug. To fix it, you could drag the octopus away from the corner before starting, but it's better to use a script that moves it automatically. Insert a "go to" block at the start of the script for Octopus2 to send it to the centre of the stage.

●● **LINGO**

Bugs

A bug is an error in a program. The first computers made mistakes when real insects, or bugs, got in their circuits. The name stuck. Today, programmers often spend as much time finding and fixing bugs as they do writing code in the first place.

Octopus2 can trap the player in the top-right corner.

Add this block to make Octopus2 start in the centre of the stage.

△ **Fine-tuning**

The best games have been carefully tested to make sure they play well. Test every change you make and get friends to play your games to see how well they work.

▽ Different colours

Make your octopuses different colours by using the "set colour" block from the Looks section. Place it under the "set size" block at the start of the script.

Try setting this number anywhere from −100 to 100 to see the full range of colours.

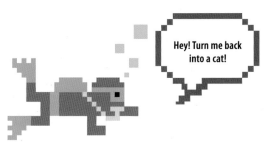

Hey! Turn me back into a cat!

△ Scuba diver

To make the underwater theme more convincing, replace the cat with a diver. Click on the cat in the sprites list, then open the Costumes tab and click on the sprite symbol ♦ to open the library. Load the costume called "diver1".

▽ Flashing colours

You can make an octopus change colour continually to create a flashing effect. Add the script below to any octopus. Try experimenting with different numbers in the "change colour" block.

Change this number to make colours change faster or slower.

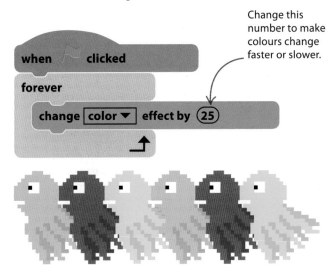

▽ Play with size

You can change how easy the game is by adjusting the size of the sprites. Change the number in the octopuses' blue "move" blocks to alter their speed. Change the purple "set size" blocks to make sprites larger or smaller. Fine-tune the numbers until the game is just hard enough to be fun.

◁ Swimming animation

To add a professional touch to Star Hunter, animate the octopuses so they look like they're swimming. Add this script to an empty part of the scripts area for each octopus to make them switch between two different poses.

Cheese
Chase

How to build Cheese Chase

Some of the world's earliest and most popular computer games were maze games. In a maze game, quick thinking is essential as you race around tight corners, avoiding monsters and collecting goodies.

AIM OF THE GAME

Mimi the mouse is hungry and stuck in a maze. Help her to find the cheese, but avoid the evil beetles. And watch out for ghosts – the maze is haunted!

◁ **Mimi**
You play the game as the mouse. Use the arrow keys on your keyboard to make her run either up, down, left, or right.

◁ **Beetles**
Beetles scuttle along the edges and make random turns when they hit a wall.

◁ **Ghosts**
Ghosts can float through walls. They can appear anywhere without warning and then disappear.

Only the ghosts can move through walls.

Cheese Chase
by SuperMimi (unshared)

Score   30

The beetles are small enough to let the mouse squeeze past.

Click the green flag
to start a new game.

Click the
stop sign to
end a game.

GAME CONTROLS

Players use the arrow
keys on a keyboard
as game controls.

High Score   90

The game remembers
the highest score. Can
you beat it?

Collect blocks of cheese
to score points.

◁ **Chase the cheese**

There are countless ways to
change Cheese Chase and
create your very own version
of the game. For instance, you
can adjust the speed, increase
the number of beetles, and
change the shape of the maze.

You can create a
maze with any
pattern of walls.

Keyboard control

Many games let the player use the keyboard to control the action. In Cheese Chase, the player uses the arrow keys on their keyboard to move Mimi the mouse around the stage. Start by creating a keyboard control script for Mimi.

1 Start Scratch and choose "New Project". Delete the cat by right-clicking and selecting "delete". If you use a Mac computer, instead of right-clicking you can hold down the control key and click.

2 Click the "New sprite" symbol and look through the sprite library for Mouse1. Click "OK". The mouse should now be on the stage and in the sprites list.

Click here to open the sprite library.

The mouse is highlighted in blue to show it's your current sprite.

3 Add this script to the mouse to move the sprite up the stage using the up arrow key. To find the different coloured blocks, remember to click the different options in the Scripts tab. Read through the script carefully and think about what it does. Run the script by clicking the green flag. You should be able to move the Mouse sprite up the stage using the up arrow key.

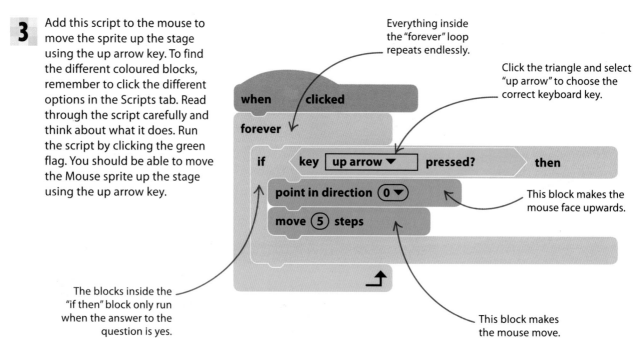

Everything inside the "forever" loop repeats endlessly.

Click the triangle and select "up arrow" to choose the correct keyboard key.

This block makes the mouse face upwards.

The blocks inside the "if then" block only run when the answer to the question is yes.

This block makes the mouse move.

4 To make the other arrow keys work, add three more "if then" blocks like the first one, but choose a different arrow key and direction for each one. To move right, select the right arrow key and set the direction to 90. For down, set it to 180. For left, set it to –90. Read through the finished script to make sure you understand it.

Each "if then" block should be inside the "forever" loop, but not inside any of the other "if then" blocks.

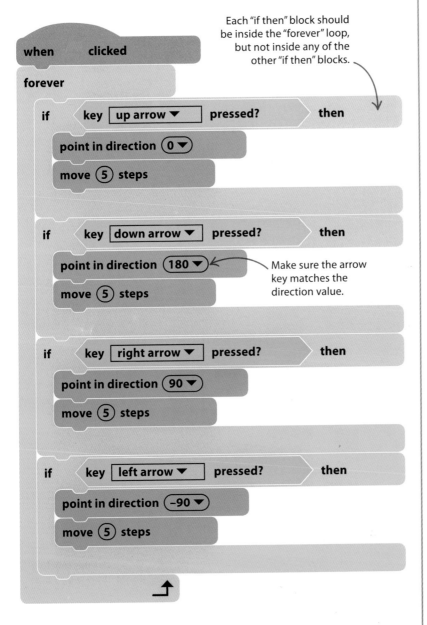

when clicked

forever

if key up arrow ▼ pressed? then

point in direction 0 ▼

move 5 steps

if key down arrow ▼ pressed? then

point in direction 180 ▼

Make sure the arrow key matches the direction value.

move 5 steps

if key right arrow ▼ pressed? then

point in direction 90 ▼

move 5 steps

if key left arrow ▼ pressed? then

point in direction –90 ▼

move 5 steps

5 Now click the green flag to run the script. You should be able to move the mouse in all directions around the stage using the arrow keys. If it's not working, go back and check all the steps.

▪ ▪ GAME DESIGN
Controllers

In Cheese Chase, we use the arrow keys to control the game, and in Star Hunter we used the mouse. Other computer games use very different types of controller.

▷ Console controller

Console controllers usually have two small joysticks controlled with your thumbs, along with a range of other buttons. They are ideal for complex games that need a lot of different controls.

▷ Dance mats

You control the game by stepping on giant keys. Dance mats are good for games involving physical activity, but they don't give fine control.

▷ Motion sensor

These controllers detect movement, which makes them ideal for sports games where you swing your arms to use a racquet or bat, for example.

▷ Camera

Special cameras in some game consoles allow the player to use body movements to control the game.

Using the paint editor

Cheese Chase now has its mouse heroine and she's hungry, but there's no cheese yet for her to chase. The sprite library in Scratch doesn't include a picture of cheese, so you'll need to make one yourself. You can do this with Scratch's paint editor.

My cheese piece is a masterpiece!

6 Create a blank sprite by clicking the small paintbrush symbol above the sprites list. This will open Scratch's paint editor in a screen like the one below. Make sure "Bitmap Mode" is selected at the bottom.

Undo
Redo
Crop
Flip
Use this tool to set the centre of the sprite.

costume1 — Clear — Add — Import

Paintbrush tool
Straight line tool
Rectangle tool
Circle tool

Use this tool to fill a shape with colour.

Use this tool to select part of a drawing.

Eraser

Use this tool to duplicate part of a drawing.

Outline
Solid
Colour palette

Line thickness

100%

Bitmap Mode
Convert to vector

7 Now draw the cheese. Use the paintbrush tool and choose black from the colour palette at the bottom of the screen. Draw the outline of the cheese. If you want perfectly straight lines, use the line tool. Your cheese drawing might be too big at first, but you can make it smaller later.

Use this tool to draw wiggly lines.

Use this tool to draw straight lines.

8 If you like, use the circle tool to draw holes in the cheese. Make the circle an outline rather than a solid circle by choosing the outline option at the bottom.

Use this tool to draw holes.

9 To add colour, choose yellow and use the fill tool to fill in the cheese. If your colour spills out and fills the whole background, click on the "undo" button. Make sure your lines don't have any gaps, then try again.

Select this tool and click inside the shape to fill it with colour.

The background should stay this pattern to show it's transparent.

10 Now set the centre of your cheese. Click the "Set costume centre" tool in the top right and then click the middle of the cheese. The cheese is now ready to be added to the game.

Select this tool and click in the middle of the cheese.

11 To keep score, we need to create a variable called "Score". Choose Data in the blocks palette and click on "Make a Variable". Type the word "Score" in the pop-up box. The score counter will now appear on the stage.

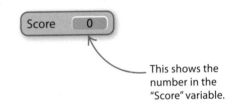

This shows the number in the "Score" variable.

12 Now add a script to make the cheese appear in a random location. When the mouse touches it, there will be a "pop" noise, the player will score ten points, and the cheese will move to a new location. Run the script and try catching the cheese. It should be easy – but that's because you haven't added enemies yet...

This block moves the Cheese sprite to random locations around the stage.

The script pauses here until the mouse arrives.

Getting spooky

Adding our first enemy to the project will make Cheese Chase into a proper game. A ghost is a good first enemy for this game because it can float through walls, so you won't need to change the ghost's script when we add the maze.

13 Click the "New sprite" symbol and select a ghost sprite from the sprite library. Click "OK" to add it to the project.

New sprite:

Click here to open the library.

The ghost is now your selected sprite.

Ghost1

14 Add the following script to the ghost to make it chase the mouse. If it touches the mouse, the game will end. You might recognize most of this code from Star Hunter.

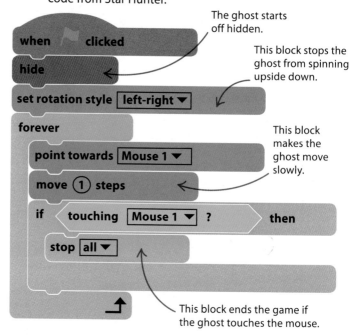

The ghost starts off hidden.

when ⚑ clicked

hide

This block stops the ghost from spinning upside down.

set rotation style [left-right ▼]

forever

point towards [Mouse 1 ▼]

This block makes the ghost move slowly.

move (1) steps

if ⟨ touching [Mouse 1 ▼] ? ⟩ then

stop [all ▼]

This block ends the game if the ghost touches the mouse.

Starts a new script. Ghost1 will now have two scripts.

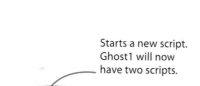

when clicked

forever

hide

This block keeps the ghost hidden for 5–10 seconds.

wait pick random (5) to (10) secs

go to x: pick random (−220) to (220) y: pick random (−160) to (160)

show

wait pick random (3) to (6) secs

15 Now add a separate script to make the ghost appear and disappear for random amounts of time. The "hide" block makes the sprite disappear, and "show" makes it appear again.

This block makes the ghost appear in a random place on the stage.

This block keeps the ghost on screen for 3–6 seconds.

16 Next add music to the game. We usually add music to the stage rather than a sprite. Click the stage area on the left of the sprites list to highlight it in blue. Click the Scripts tab and add the following script to play a sound over and over. Click Sound in the blocks palette to find the "play sound until done" block.

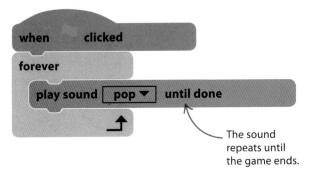

The sound repeats until the game ends.

17 Now click the Sounds tab above the blocks palette. Click the speaker symbol to open the sound library. Select the category "Music Loops" on the left, then choose the music "xylo1" and click "OK". Repeat the process to load "dance celebrate" into the game too.

Sounds tab

This opens the sound library.

18 Return to the Scripts tab and change the selected sound from "pop" to "xylo1". Run the game and think about how it feels to play. Next try the sound "dance celebrate". Which one is better?

Click the triangle to choose the sound.

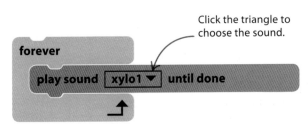

. . GAME DESIGN

Music in games

Watch a scary film with the sound off and it's not so scary anymore. Games are the same – the music sets the mood. A fast-paced game will use music with a driving beat to make you hurry. A spooky game should have haunting music to make you feel uneasy – jolly, bouncy music would break the spell. A puzzle game might have echoing, eerie music to create a sense of mystery. Some games use music as a key part of the game play, such as those where the player has to dance or push buttons in time to the beat.

You never know where I'll appear next!

Maze making

Mimi the mouse can run anywhere she likes on the stage. Put a stop to that by adding a maze. The maze will make it difficult for her to move from one place to another, adding an extra challenge to Cheese Chase.

This opens the paint editor.

19 The maze will be a sprite, not a backdrop, because that makes it easier to detect when another sprite touches it. Draw it in Scratch's paint editor. Click on the paintbrush symbol in the sprites list, then click on the blue "i" and rename the sprite "Maze".

Name this sprite "Cheese".

Rename the sprite "Maze".

20 Now you can start using the paint editor. Make sure "Bitmap Mode" is selected in the bottom right. If not, click the "Convert to bitmap" button to change the mode. Choose the line tool and set the line width control to the middle. Then pick a dark colour for the maze walls.

Draw the maze in the empty space here.

costume1 | Clear | Add | Import

Line tool

Choose a colour before you start drawing.

Select "Bitmap Mode" before you draw the maze.

Slide the line width control to the middle.

100%

Bitmap Mode

Convert to vector

21 Now draw the maze. Start by drawing the outside of the maze at the outer edge of the chequered drawing area. Hold down the shift key on your keyboard to make sure lines are perfectly vertical or horizontal. Then add the inside walls.

Make sure the lines of the maze are perfectly straight.

costume1 | Clear Add Import | 100% Bitmap Mode Convert to vector

22 Finally, we need to add a script to make sure the maze is always in the centre of the stage so it's fully visible. With the Maze sprite selected, click on the Scripts tab and add the following script.

```
when [flag] clicked
go to x: (0) y: (0)
```

At the centre of the stage, x is 0 and y is 0.

23 Run the project. You'll find that Mimi can run through walls, but don't worry as we'll fix that later.

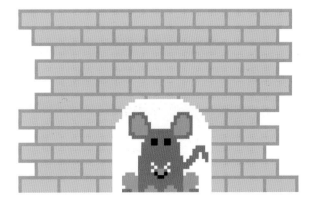

24 Mimi, the ghost, and the cheese are all too big for the maze, so we need to shrink them. Add the following blocks at the beginning of Mimi's script, before the "forever" block, and fill in the numbers below.

This makes Mimi about a third of her current size.

This sends her to the top left when the game starts.

This block makes her face right.

25 Now add a purple "set size to" block to the ghost's main script. Set the size to 35 per cent. Add a "set size to" block to the Cheese sprite too, and adjust the percentage until the cheese is about twice the size of Mimi.

Mimi is half the size of the cheese.

26 You might need to fine-tune your Maze costume to make sure Mimi can fit through all the passages, with enough room to pass her enemies (which we're going to add later). To alter the maze, select the Maze sprite and click the Costumes tab. Use the eraser tool 🧽 to remove walls or the selection tool 🖐 to move them.

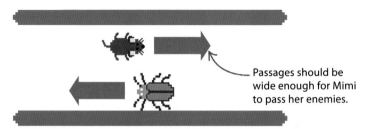

Passages should be wide enough for Mimi to pass her enemies.

27 If you use the eraser, be careful not to leave any flecks of paint behind as Mimi will stop if she hits them. Check the corners of the maze for bumps that Mimi might get stuck on and remove them.

Remove bumps with the eraser tool.

28 Add a background colour to the game by painting a backdrop, not the Maze sprite. At the bottom left of the screen, click the paintbrush symbol in the stage info area. This opens the paint editor. Make sure "Bitmap Mode" is selected at the bottom.

Click here to paint the backdrop.

29 Choose a colour, select the fill tool ◆, and then click on the backdrop to fill it with colour.

Try different colours to see which one looks best in the maze.

■ ■ **GAME DESIGN**

Space in games

How the obstacles in a game are laid out has a big effect on how you play. A maze is the perfect obstacle to demonstrate this.

Walls restrict movement.

△ **Open space**
The player can move in any direction most of the time. A game like this needs fast-moving enemies or lots of enemies to make it challenging.

△ **Closed-in space**
The player is forced to move in a very limited way. Just one enemy patrolling the corridors of this maze would make life hard. The player has to think ahead to avoid getting trapped.

△ **Balanced space**
This is what the maze in Cheese Chase is designed to be. It limits the player's movement enough to make the game interesting, but allows some freedom.

Mouse trap

Mimi can currently run straight through the walls of the maze like a ghost, but we want her to stay trapped inside the passages. Time to change her script.

Uh oh!

30 Select Mimi and drag the following blocks to an empty part of the scripts area. This set of blocks will make Mimi reverse if she runs into a wall.

if < touching [Maze ▼] ? > then
    move (–5) steps

This block makes Mimi move five steps backwards.

31 Insert the blocks four times into Mimi's main script. To make copies, right-click (or control-click if you use a Mac) on the new blocks and select "duplicate". Place the duplicates after each "move 5 steps" block.

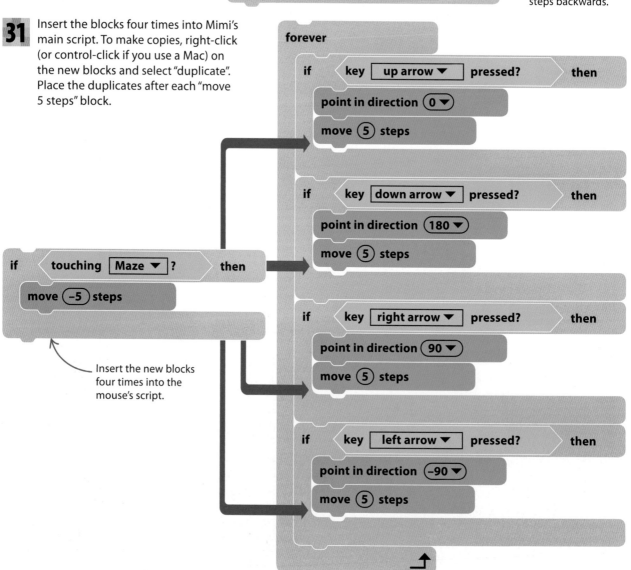

forever
    if < key [up arrow ▼] pressed? > then
        point in direction (0 ▼)
        move (5) steps

    if < key [down arrow ▼] pressed? > then
        point in direction (180 ▼)
        move (5) steps

    if < key [right arrow ▼] pressed? > then
        point in direction (90 ▼)
        move (5) steps

    if < key [left arrow ▼] pressed? > then
        point in direction (–90 ▼)
        move (5) steps

if < touching [Maze ▼] ? > then
    move (–5) steps

Insert the new blocks four times into the mouse's script.

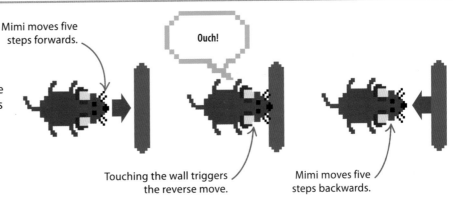

Mimi moves five steps forwards.

Ouch!

Touching the wall triggers the reverse move.

Mimi moves five steps backwards.

▷ How does it work?

You might wonder why Mimi has to move five steps backwards. The reason is that she normally moves forward five steps at a time. The backward move reverses the forward one, making her stand still. This happens so quickly that you don't see her reverse.

32 If Mimi's tail or paws touch a wall when she turns around, she can get stuck. We can fix this bug by making some changes to Mimi's costume in the paint editor.

If Mimi's tail overlaps the wall, she might stop moving.

33 Select Mouse1 in the sprites list and click the Costumes tab above the blocks palette. Choose "Convert to bitmap" at the bottom, and then use the eraser tool to trim Mimi's tail.

34 There's another problem that we can fix. Every sprite has a centre point, but if this isn't in the exact centre, the mouse will wobble when its direction changes and might overlap a wall and get stuck. Choose the "Set costume centre" tool and then click in the exact middle of Mimi to correct her centre point.

EXPERT TIPS
Bounding boxes

One of the big challenges that game programmers face is detecting when sprites with complicated shapes collide. Even in simple 2D games, collision detection can cause problems, such as sprites getting stuck or solid objects merging. A common solution is to use "bounding boxes" – invisible rectangles or circles that surround the sprite. When these simple shapes intersect, a collision is detected. In 3D games, spheres or 3D boxes can do the same job.

Set costume centre

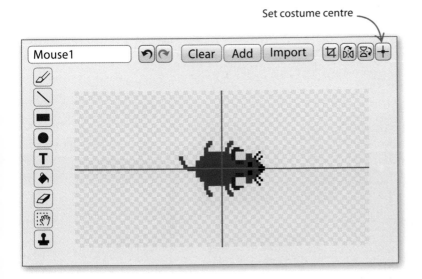

Mouse1 | Clear | Add | Import

Beetle mania

Now for Mimi's main enemies: a small army of evil beetles that scurry about inside the maze. If she bumps into one, the game ends.

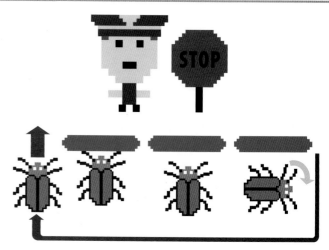

35 To make the beetles move automatically, you need to create a sequence of steps for them to follow. Programmers call this an algorithm. Our algorithm will tell each beetle to move forward until it hits a wall. Then it will stop, turn, and move forward again.

36 Click the "New sprite" symbol and choose the Beetle sprite from the library.

The beetle is now your selected sprite.

Beetle

37 Add the following script to set the beetle's size, location, and direction. It uses a "forever" loop to move the beetle, and an "if then" block to make it stop and turn right whenever it hits a wall.

You may need to change these numbers if the beetle starts on a wall.

This block makes the beetle reverse and then turn right when it hits a wall.

This block makes the beetle turn right.

38 Run the script. You might notice a glitch: the beetle always turns right and ends up going round in loops. We need to change the script so that the beetle turns left or right at random. To make a random choice, use a "pick random" block. Drag it to an empty part of the scripts area and set the second number to 2.

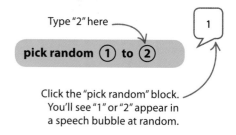

Type "2" here

pick random (1) to (2)

1

Click the "pick random" block. You'll see "1" or "2" appear in a speech bubble at random.

39 Now drag the "pick random" block into the first window of an "equal to" block. Then drag the "equal to" block into an "if then else" block.

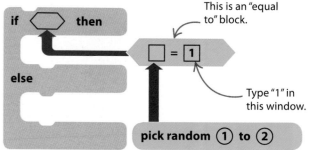

This is an "equal to" block.

if ⬡ then

else

☐ = 1

Type "1" in this window.

pick random (1) to (2)

40 Add two "turn 90 degrees" blocks to make the beetle turn left or right. Read through the script carefully and see if you can figure out how it works.

41 Remove the "turn 90 degrees" block from the beetle's original script and put the "if then else" block in its place, as below. Run the project and watch what happens. Check there's enough room for Mimi to squeeze past the beetle. If not, adjust the maze in the paint editor.

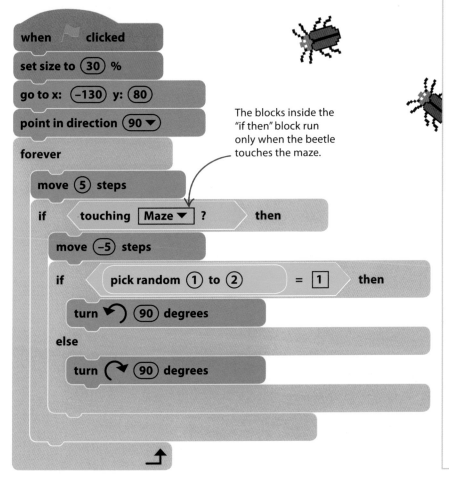

The blocks inside the "if then" block run only when the beetle touches the maze.

if then else

The "if then else" block is just like an "if then" but with an extra trick. A normal "if then" asks a question and runs the blocks inside only if the answer is yes. The "if then else" block can hold two groups of blocks: one to run if the answer is yes, and another if the answer is no. The words "if", "then", and "else" are used in nearly all computer languages to make decisions between two options.

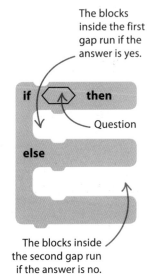

The blocks inside the first gap run if the answer is yes.

Question

The blocks inside the second gap run if the answer is no.

Sending messages

The next step is to make the beetle end the game if Mimi bumps into it. Instead of using another "touching" block in Mimi's script, you can use a message. Scratch lets you send messages between sprites to trigger scripts. The beetle will send a message to Mimi that stops her script.

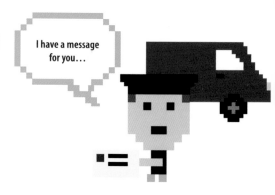

I have a message for you...

42 Add the "if then" blocks shown below to the beetle's script. The new blocks check whether the beetle is touching Mimi and, if it is, send a message. Select "Mouse1" in the "touching" block.

```
when  clicked
set size to (30) %
go to x: (−130) y: (80)
point to direction (90 ▼)
forever
    move (5) steps
    if  touching  Maze ▼ ?  then
        move (−5) steps
        if  pick random (1) to (2)  = [1]  then
            turn ↻ (90) degrees
        else
            turn ↻ (90) degrees
```

43 Now give the message a name. Open the menu in the "broadcast" block, choose "new message", and type "GameOver" in the pop-up box.

```
broadcast  message1 ▼
           message1
           new message...
```

New Message
Message Name: GameOver
OK   Cancel

Type "GameOver".

Select "Mouse1".

```
if  touching  Mouse1 ▼ ?  then
    broadcast  message 1 ▼
```

This block is found under Events. It sends a message when the beetle hits Mimi.

44 Now add an extra script to Mimi to receive the message. Drag the following blocks to an empty part of her scripts area. Try the game out. Mimi should stop moving when she touches the beetle, but the beetle will continue to move. Later we'll use a message to show a "GAME OVER!" sign as well.

This block stops Mimi's main script.

45 The game needs more beetles. Copy the Beetle sprite by right-clicking on it (use control-click if you work on a Mac) and then choose "duplicate". Make three new beetles. These will all have the same script. See what happens when you run the project.

Select "duplicate" to create new beetles.

46 You'll need to change the numbers in the "go to" blocks for each new beetle so they don't all start in the same place. Starting in different corners works quite well. Experiment!

Beetles start in corners.

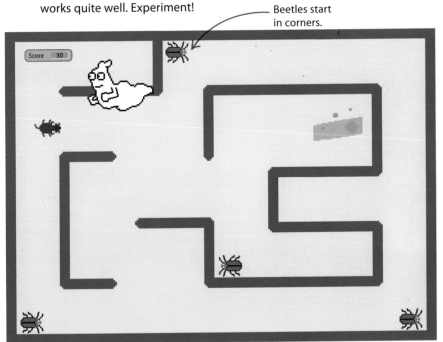

EXPERT TIPS

Messages

Messages provide a neat way of making sprites react to each other. We could have made the mouse check if it's touching a beetle, but that would mean adding "if then" and "touching" blocks to Mimi's script for all four beetles. By using messages, we can add more enemies without changing Mimi's code.

High score

You can make a game more fun by adding a high score for players to beat. We create this in the same way as the score tracker: by making a variable and displaying it on the stage.

47 Select Data in the blocks palette. Click "Make a Variable" and create a new variable called "High Score". A new block will appear, and the high score counter will appear on the stage. Drag it wherever you like.

New Variable

Variable name: High Score

● For all sprites   ○ For this sprite only

OK   Cancel

48 Now add an extra set of blocks to the Cheese sprite's "forever" loop to test for a new high score each time the player gains points. Run the project and see if anyone can beat your high score.

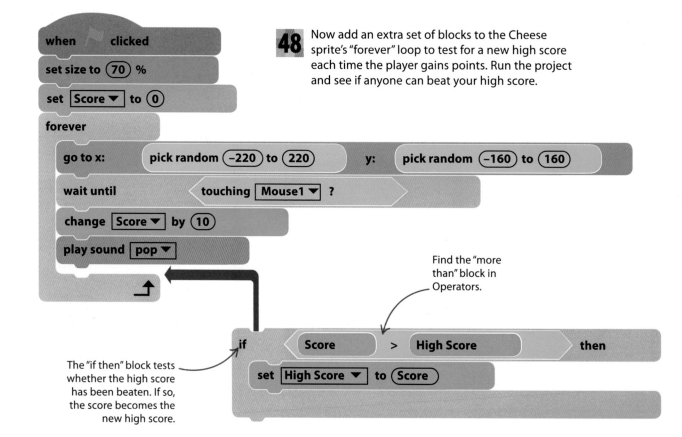

```
when   clicked
set size to (70) %
set  Score ▼  to (0)
forever
    go to x:  pick random (-220) to (220)   y:   pick random (-160) to (160)
    wait until       touching  Mouse1 ▼  ?
    change  Score ▼  by (10)
    play sound  pop ▼
```

Find the "more than" block in Operators.

```
if      Score      >   High Score      then
    set  High Score ▼  to (Score)
```

The "if then" block tests whether the high score has been beaten. If so, the score becomes the new high score.

Game over!

At the moment, the only signal the game has ended is that the mouse stops moving. You can add a finishing touch to any game by displaying a large, bold "GAME OVER!" sign. To do this you need to create a sprite and use the "GameOver" message to make it appear.

Don't forget to check the sprite's centre with the set centre tool.

49 Click the paintbrush symbol ✐ in the sprites list to create a new sprite with the paint editor. Using "Bitmap Mode", draw a rectangle and fill it with a dark colour. Now switch to "Vector Mode". Choose a bright colour and use the text tool to type "GAME OVER!" in the rectangle. Change the font to "Scratch" and use the selection tool to make the text large.

Use the selection tool to enlarge the text.

To change the font, highlight the text first.

Change the font to Scratch.

50 You don't want the "GAME OVER!" sign to show until the game is really over, so let's hide it with a script. Switch to the Scripts tab and add these blocks.

when ⚑ clicked
hide

51 Now add a script to make the sprite appear when the game ends. You can use the same message that stops Mimi to trigger this script.

This places the "GAME OVER!" sign in the middle.

when I receive GameOver ▼
go to x: 0 y: 0
go to front
show

This block ensures other sprites are behind the sign.

52 Run the game. You should now see the "GAME OVER!" sign when you get caught by a beetle. To make the sign work with the ghost too, replace its "stop all" block with a "broadcast GameOver" block.

Hacks and tweaks

Take Cheese Chase to the next level by tweaking the rules of the game and the way the sprites behave. You can also experiment with big changes that turn Cheese Chase into a totally different kind of game.

◁ **Play on**
You need to play the game a lot to find out what works and what can be improved. Get other people to play. You can adjust many properties of the game until you get the right configuration: a game where the abilities of the player and enemies are well balanced.

△ **Add sounds**
Jazz up the game with some sound effects using the "play sounds" block when the ghost appears, when the game ends, or when you get a high score. There are lots of sounds in Scratch's sound library that you can experiment with.

▷ **Tweak timings**
You might find Cheese Chase harder than Star Hunter. To make it easier, you can make the beetles slower or make the ghost appear for a shorter time. You can also speed up Mimi. For variety, try making each beetle run at a different speed.

▷ **Rocket power**
Add a power boost that hides all the enemies for ten seconds when the mouse touches it. To do this, you would need to add a new sprite and a message to trigger a hide-wait-show script in each enemy.

▽ **Vanishing cheese**
For an extra challenge, make the cheese spend only ten seconds or so in each spot before moving to a new location. This will force the player to move fast. To do this, give the cheese an extra script with a "forever" loop containing a "wait 10 secs" block, followed by a copy of the "go to" block from the main script.

This block picks a random location for the cheese.

▷ Don't touch the walls

Make the game end if Mimi touches the walls of the maze. Add a script to the Maze sprite to send the message "GameOver" if she touches the maze. This makes the game much harder. To make it even harder, try switching the player's controls from the keyboard to the computer mouse. The game then becomes a test of a steady hand.

Adding instructions

Players like to see a game's instructions clearly before they start playing. Here are three ways of including instructions.

▽ Project page

The easiest way to include instructions is to simply type them in the instructions box on the project page. You need to log in to an online Scratch account to do this.

Type the instructions here.

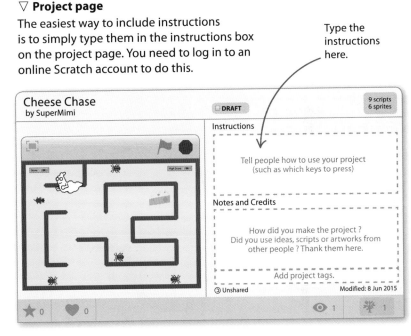

▽ Instructions sprite

You can use the paint editor to create an Instructions sprite in the same way that you created the game-over sprite. Give it the following script to show the sprite at the start of the game and to hide it once the player presses the space bar.

```
when   clicked
go to x: (0) y: (0)
go to front
show
wait until    key  space ▼  pressed ?
hide
```

The Instructions sprite appears until you press the space bar.

```
when   clicked
set size to (35) %
wait until    key  space ▼  pressed ?
```

Add this "wait until" block to the start of every other sprite's script so they don't start moving until the game begins.

▽ Speech bubbles

Make your game characters tell the player the instructions using speech bubbles. Add a "say" block to the start of Mimi's script to explain the game. Don't forget to add "wait" blocks to the enemies' scripts – otherwise there's a risk you'll lose before you start!

Do as I say!

Circle
Wars

How to build Circle Wars

Lightning reactions are essential in Circle Wars, a fast-paced game in which you hunt green circles while being chased by red ones. The game uses Scratch's clones feature, which can turn a single sprite into an army of sinister copies.

AIM OF THE GAME

Move the blue circle around the screen using the mouse. Collect the pale green circles, but avoid the red ones that march towards you like a zombie army. The solid green and solid red circles drop clones of themselves as they roam around. Score more than 20 points to win and go below −20 to lose.

◁ **Player**
The player is the blue circle. If you don't keep moving quickly, the enemy circles will soon overwhelm you.

◁ **Friends**
The friendly circles are green. When you touch one, you score a point and the circle disappears with a pop.

◁ **Enemies**
Steer clear of the red enemy circles. Touch one and it takes three points off your score, before vanishing with a clash of cymbals.

The timer shows how long each game takes.

The score rises or falls as green and red clones are touched by the player.

Circle Wars
by HappyShrimp321 (unshared)

Score 8

Time 23.5

The solid green circle lays the friendly clones.

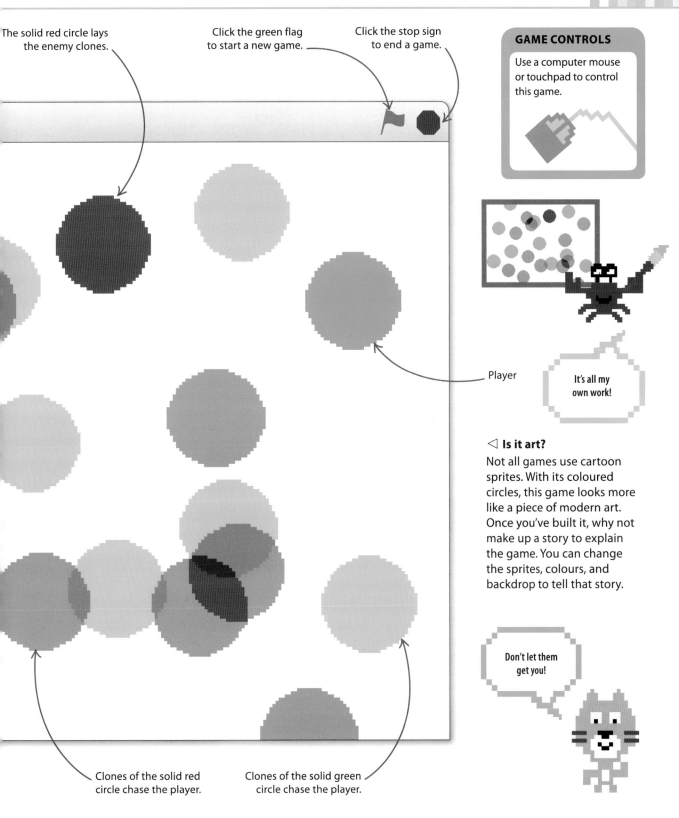

The solid red circle lays the enemy clones.

Click the green flag to start a new game.

Click the stop sign to end a game.

GAME CONTROLS

Use a computer mouse or touchpad to control this game.

Player

It's all my own work!

◁ **Is it art?**

Not all games use cartoon sprites. With its coloured circles, this game looks more like a piece of modern art. Once you've built it, why not make up a story to explain the game. You can change the sprites, colours, and backdrop to tell that story.

Don't let them get you!

Clones of the solid red circle chase the player.

Clones of the solid green circle chase the player.

Creating the sprites

First you need to create the three sprites for the main game. These are all simple coloured circles, so you can draw them yourself. Start by following these instructions to create the player's character – the blue circle.

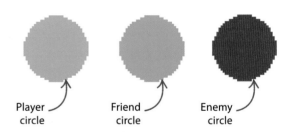

Player circle   Friend circle   Enemy circle

1 Start a new project and name it "Circle Wars". Click the paintbrush symbol at the top of the sprites list to paint a new sprite.

New sprite:

Click here to paint a new sprite.

2 To draw a blue circle, first select "Bitmap Mode" (bottom right). Then choose blue in the colour palette.

Circle tool

3 Click the circle tool on the left and then select a solid colour (rather than an outline) at the bottom left of the paint editor.

Select solid colour.

4 While holding down the shift key (this gives you a circle rather than an oval), click with the mouse and drag to draw a circle. The circle should be about the size of the cat's head. When you're happy with the circle's size, delete the cat sprite (right-click on it and select "delete").

Look on the stage to compare the size of your new sprite to the cat.

5 You now need to centre the sprite. Select the "Set costume centre" tool (top right) and then click in the very centre of the circle. Rename the sprite "Player" by clicking on the blue "i" in the sprites list.

EXPERT TIPS
Resizing the circle

If your circle is too big or too small, you can change the size of it by selecting either the "Grow" or "Shrink" tool on the bar along the top of the Scratch screen, then clicking on the circle.

Grow

Shrink

Making friends and enemies

You can now make the green friend and red enemy circles. You can use other colours if you like, but make sure you can easily tell the three different circles apart.

Selecting "duplicate" makes a copy of the sprite.

6 Start by right-clicking on the Player sprite and selecting "duplicate". Do this twice. You'll now have three blue circles. Rename Player2 as "Friends" and Player3 as "Enemies".

7 Select the Friends sprite and click the Costumes tab. Choose green in the colour palette. Select the "Fill with color" tool and click inside the blue circle to make it turn green.

"Fill with color" tool

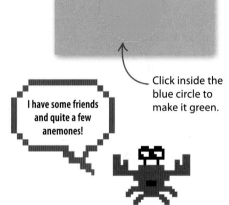

Click inside the blue circle to make it green.

8 Repeat the steps for the Enemies sprite, but colour this sprite red. You should now have three different coloured sprites.

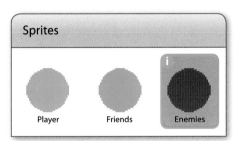

I have some friends and quite a few anemones!

Instant player control

Now add a score display and a script to make the Player sprite stick to the mouse-pointer – just like in Star Hunter.

9 Select the Player sprite, click Data, and make a variable called "Score" for all sprites. Then tick the variable's check box to show "Score" on the stage.

New Variable

Variable name: | Score

● For all sprites   ○ For this sprite only

OK   Cancel

Ticking this box ensures that the score will appear on the stage.

☑ **Score**

10 Add the script below to get the blue circle following the mouse. Read it through and make sure you understand what it does. Run the script to check it works. The red and green circles won't do anything yet.

```
when [flag] clicked
set [Score ▼] to [0]
forever
    go to [mouse-pointer ▼]
```

This block "glues" the Player sprite to the mouse-pointer.

March of the clones

From just two sprites – the green and red circles – you can create an army of friends and enemies to pursue the player's blue circle. You can do this through the magic of cloning. Before you create your clones, first get the Friends sprite moving randomly around the stage.

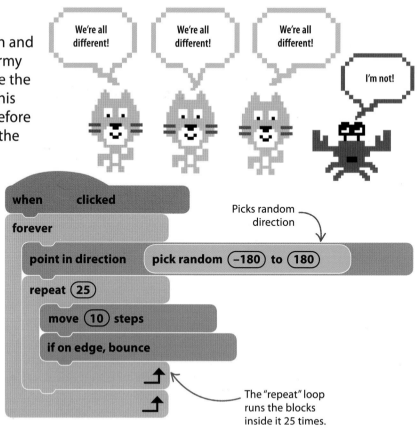

We're all different!

We're all different!

We're all different!

I'm not!

11 Select the green Friends sprite. Add this script to make the circle bounce around the stage with a random change of direction every 250 steps.

Picks random direction

```
when clicked
forever
    point in direction (pick random (-180) to (180))
    repeat (25)
        move (10) steps
        if on edge, bounce
```

The "repeat" loop runs the blocks inside it 25 times.

12 Run the project and watch the green circle's unpredictable journey. The Friends sprite moves 250 steps in 10-step jumps but it doesn't get stuck to the walls. After 250 steps, the "forever" loop goes back to the start. The sprite changes direction randomly and sets off again.

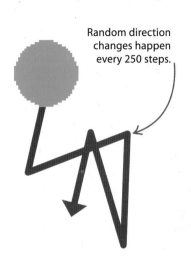

Random direction changes happen every 250 steps.

Repeat loops

You've already seen "forever" loops that repeat a group of blocks nonstop. A "repeat" loop does a similar job, but it only repeats the blocks inside a fixed number of times. This type of loop is sometimes called a "for" loop, because it repeats *for* a certain number of times. The example shown here repeats an action four times to draw a square.

The blocks inside repeat 4 times.

```
when clicked
pen down
repeat (4)
    move (100) steps
    turn ↻ (90) degrees
pen up
```

After 4 repeats, the next block is run.

Making clones

Now we're going to make our friendly clone army. These are the clones you need to catch to score points.

13 Add a "create clone of myself" block as the last block in the "forever" loop. You'll find it in the yellow Control section. This block will create a clone of the Friends sprite after each 250-step movement.

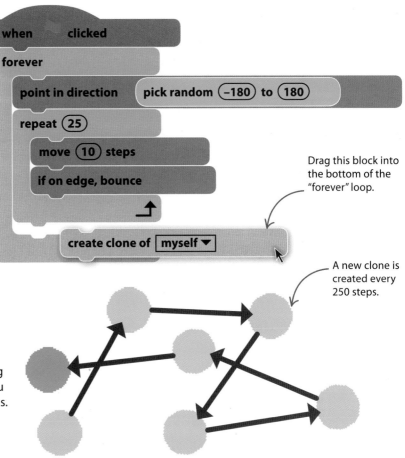

when ⚑ clicked
forever
  point in direction pick random -180 to 180
  repeat 25
    move 10 steps
    if on edge, bounce
  create clone of myself ▼

Drag this block into the bottom of the "forever" loop.

A new clone is created every 250 steps.

14 Run the project. At each change of direction, the sprite leaves a copy of itself – a clone. The clones aren't just pictures – they are fully working copies of the original sprite, and you can give them their own instructions.

15 New clones are controlled by a special script that starts with the block "when I start as a clone". Add the script below to the Friends sprite. The script tells each clone to move towards the Player sprite for 300 steps, after which the clone is deleted and vanishes from the stage. The clones move one step at a time. They move more slowly than the original Friends sprite, which moves in 10-step jumps.

16 Run the script and watch the green clones advance slowly towards the Player sprite. Don't worry – they're the good guys!

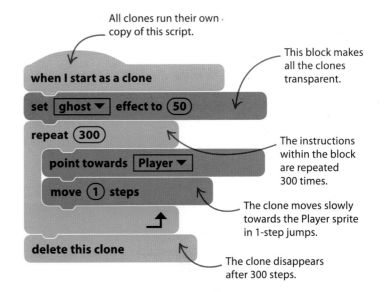

All clones run their own copy of this script.

when I start as a clone
set ghost ▼ effect to 50
repeat 300
  point towards Player ▼
  move 1 steps
delete this clone

This block makes all the clones transparent.

The instructions within the block are repeated 300 times.

The clone moves slowly towards the Player sprite in 1-step jumps.

The clone disappears after 300 steps.

Destroying clones

The last part of the script for the Friends clone checks if the clone is touching the Player. If it is, the clone gets deleted.

17 Add an "if then" block containing the blocks shown here to check whether the clone is touching the Player sprite after each move. Try running the project now – the score should rise as you touch green circles, which instantly disappear with a pop.

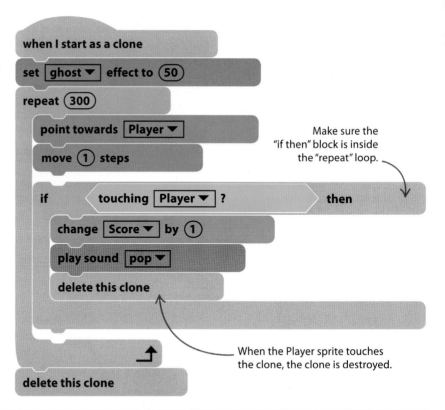

```
when I start as a clone

set  ghost ▾  effect to  50

repeat  300
    point towards  Player ▾
    move  1  steps
    if          touching  Player ▾  ?          then
        change  Score ▾  by  1
        play sound  pop ▾
        delete this clone

delete this clone
```

Make sure the "if then" block is inside the "repeat" loop.

When the Player sprite touches the clone, the clone is destroyed.

POP!

Clones

Clones are useful any time you want lots of copies of a sprite. Many programming languages let you make copies of things, but they are often called objects rather than clones.

Such languages are called "object oriented" languages and include Java and C++. In Scratch, there are three orange blocks that control clones, all found in the Control section.

```
create clone of  myself ▾
```

△ This block creates a clone of the sprite. The clone is identical to the sprite and appears in the same position and facing the same direction, so you won't be able to see it until it moves.

```
when I start as a clone
```

△ When a clone starts, it runs the script headed with this block. Clones don't run the sprite's main script, but they can run all other scripts in the sprite's scripts area, such as scripts triggered by messages.

```
delete this clone
```

△ This block gets rid of the clone. All clones disappear from the stage when a project stops, leaving just the original sprite.

Enemy clones

Now you need to add scripts to the Enemies sprite to make it produce clones that chase the Player. You can do this by copying the scripts from the Friends sprite across to the Enemies sprite.

18 To copy scripts, just click, drag, and drop scripts from one sprite onto another. Drag the two scripts you made for the Friends sprite onto the Enemies sprite, one at a time. This makes copies of the scripts in the Enemies sprite.

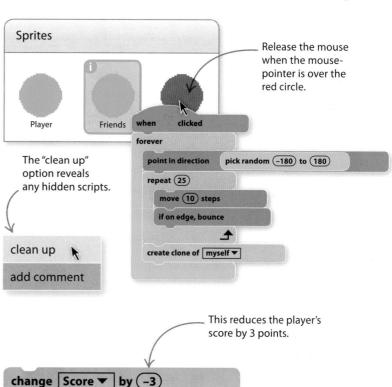

Release the mouse when the mouse-pointer is over the red circle.

Sprites

Player   Friends

The "clean up" option reveals any hidden scripts.

```
when     clicked
forever
    point in direction   pick random (-180) to (180)
    repeat (25)
        move (10) steps
        if on edge, bounce
    create clone of [ myself ▼ ]
```

clean up

add comment

19 Select the Enemies sprite. The scripts you dragged and dropped will probably be on top of one another, because any copied script just appears at the top left of the scripts area. To rearrange them, right-click on the background and select "clean up".

20 Now adjust the Enemies clone script so that it takes points away when the Player touches a red clone. Alter the "change Score by" block so it changes the score by –3 instead of +1. You really want to avoid those nasty red enemies!

This reduces the player's score by 3 points.

```
change [ Score ▼ ] by (-3)
```

21 Add a sound to tell the player that points have been lost. Load the cymbal sound into the Enemies sprite by selecting "cymbal" in the sound library. Alter the script to play "cymbal", not "pop". You'll now hear which type of clone you've touched.

Change the script to play a cymbal sound.

```
play sound [ cymbal ▼ ]
```

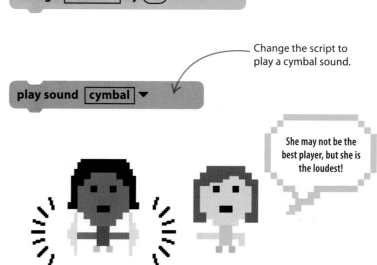

She may not be the best player, but she is the loudest!

22 Run the project. Check that you now have both red and green clones, and that touching a red clone takes 3 points off your score.

Win or lose?

You've created two ever-expanding clone armies: one of friendly circles that help you win points, and one of evil circles that make you lose points. Next you need to add the code that tells you if you've won or lost the game.

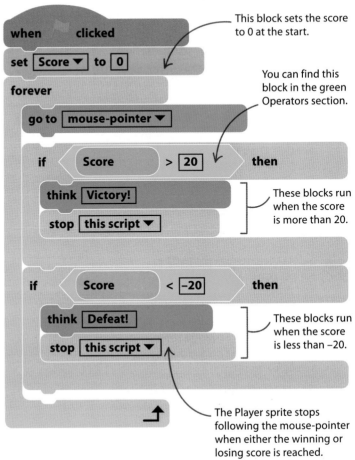

This block sets the score to 0 at the start.

You can find this block in the green Operators section.

These blocks run when the score is more than 20.

These blocks run when the score is less than −20.

The Player sprite stops following the mouse-pointer when either the winning or losing score is reached.

23 Add the new "if then" blocks shown here to the Player sprite. They check your score. If the score is greater than 20, you win, and a thought bubble with the word "Victory!" appears. If the score is less than −20, you lose, and the sprite thinks "Defeat!"

Comparison operators

Earlier we saw how you can use "if then" blocks to create true or false statements – also known as Boolean expressions – that lead to different outcomes. For example, in Star Hunter, "if touching cat then play sound fairydust" makes a sound play only when the cat gets a star. We can do the same thing with numbers by using what are called comparison operators:

When we add these to "if then" blocks, they create statements that are either true or false. In Circle Wars, the "is more than" operator tells you that you've won the game when you score over 20.

$2 < 5$	$3 = 3$	$5 > 1$
is less than	**equals**	**is more than**

24 Run the game. Try to touch only the green circles. Check that the game ends when the key scores are reached, and check that the Player sprite thinks "Victory!" or "Defeat!" You can reduce the score needed to win if you find it too difficult. But don't make the game too easy – Circle Wars is meant to be a challenge!

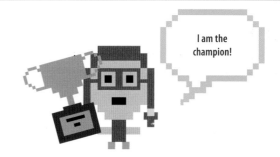

I am the champion!

Adding a timer

To add some competition to the game, you can include an on-screen timer that shows players how long they take to complete a game.

25 Click on the Data section and make a variable "Time" for all sprites. To show it on the stage, tick the box next to the variable's block. Select the Player sprite. Click on Sensing in the blocks palette. Add "reset timer" to the Player's script, just before the "forever" loop. Go back to Data and drag a "set Time to" block to the script and add "timer" to it, making it the last instruction in the forever loop.

26 By copying "timer" to the variable "Time", each trip around the loop will now display the time on the stage. But the moment the player wins or loses, the time stops being updated (the script is stopped) and the total time it took to win or lose is shown.

This block starts the timing from 0.

This block updates the Time display every time the loop repeats.

Time 41.573

Total number of seconds in the game

I think it must be lunch time!

Instructions

Players need to know the rules of the game. Create a special sprite that shows the instructions for Circle Wars when the game begins.

Use black for the text.

Choosing a light background colour will make the text easier to read.

27 Use the paintbrush symbol to create a new sprite and rename it "Instructions". Select "Bitmap Mode" and choose a colour. Select the "Fill with colour" tool and click on the drawing area to fill it with your chosen colour.

"Fill with color" tool

You may want to decorate your instructions with coloured circles.

28 Now select black from the palette as the colour for the text. Then choose the text tool and type out the instructions shown here.

Text tool

You are the blue circle.
Move using the mouse.
Be quick!

Try to touch the friendly green circles.
Each one gives you 1 point.
Avoid the enemy red circles.
Each one you touch takes 3 points.

Score more than 20 to win.
Score less than −20 and you lose.

Press the space bar to start!

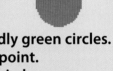

29 If the text doesn't fit, use the select tool to resize it by pulling the corner points in or out. When you've finished, click outside the box around the text to stop editing.

"Select" tool

Game stories

Computer games usually have a story to explain why the action in the game is happening. At the moment, Circle Wars has no story. Can you make one up? It could be a battle in space, with a blue spaceship saving friendly green spaceships and trying to avoid being hit by the red enemy craft. Let your imagination run riot! Including some of the story in your instructions will help to make the game more interesting and exciting for the player.

30 Add this script to the sprite to show the instructions on the stage at the start of the game. Read it carefully. Can you see how it works?

These blocks show the instructions in the centre of the screen in front of other sprites.

This block hides the Instruction sprite when the player presses the space bar to start playing.

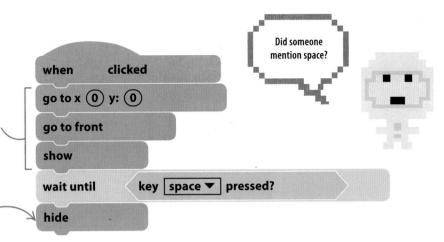

Did someone mention space?

```
when  clicked
go to x (0) y: (0)
go to front
show
wait until    key [ space ▼ ] pressed?
hide
```

31 You also need to add a "wait until key space pressed" block immediately after the green flag blocks in the Player, Friends, and Enemies sprites' scripts. This will hold back all the action until the space bar is pressed.

32 Run the project and your instructions should appear, filling the screen until you press the space bar. Players will have plenty of time to read and understand the instructions, letting them start the game when they're ready.

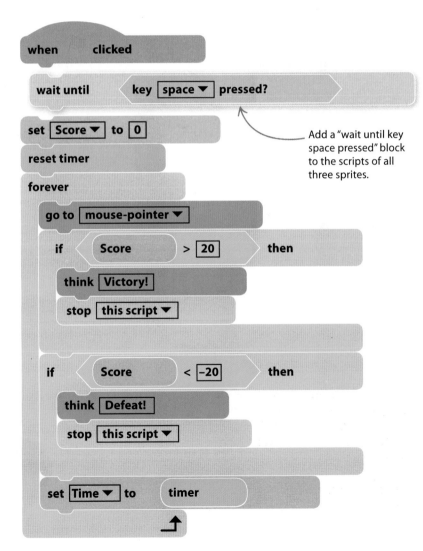

```
when  clicked
wait until    key [ space ▼ ] pressed?
set [ Score ▼ ] to [ 0 ]
reset timer
forever
    go to [ mouse-pointer ▼ ]
    if < Score > [ 20 ] > then
        think [ Victory! ]
        stop [ this script ▼ ]
    if < Score < [ -20 ] > then
        think [ Defeat! ]
        stop [ this script ▼ ]
    set [ Time ▼ ] to ( timer )
```

Add a "wait until key space pressed" block to the scripts of all three sprites.

I'm ready to play!

Hacks and tweaks

You've got Circle Wars working – well done!
Now to personalize it and make it your own.
Try these suggestions and your own ideas.
Once you've created something unique, why
not share it on the Scratch projects website?

△ **Find a balance**

Experiment with different speeds, or change
how many points you win or lose for touching
Friends and Enemies. It's not difficult to make
the game very hard or very easy, but can you
find a balance to make it just the right level?

▽ **What's the story?**

Did you think of a story to explain what's going on in
Circle Wars? Maybe it's the attack of the dragons, and
the princess player has to eat cakes to survive? Add
some scenery and music to the game to fit with that
story. Experiment with different stories and looks.

▷ **The war's over!**

Add a broadcast message to
reveal a game-over sprite when
the player wins or loses, like you
did in Cheese Chase. You can
change the text of the game-over
sprite so that it relates to your
story about the game.

▷ **Slow down, blue!**

To make things tricky, change
the blue circle's script so that it
no longer "sticks" to the mouse
pointer but chases slowly after
it. You could also invent simple
keyboard controls for the sprite.

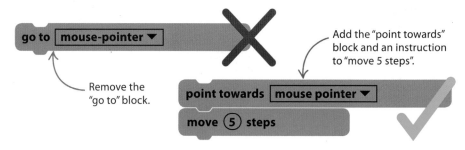

Remove the
"go to" block.

Add the "point towards"
block and an instruction
to "move 5 steps".

▽ **Tweak the timer**

The number in the timer flickers because it shows lots of
decimal places. To round the value so it shows only whole
seconds, use the green "round" block near the bottom of
the Operators section. Try adding a "Best time" for winning
players, just as you added a "High score" in Cheese Chase.

That's their best
time yet!

▽ **Change the colours**

Vary the clones' colours. Click on the Friends sprite. Add the "set color effect to" block from the Looks section to the sprite's clone script. Then drag "pick random" from Operators into the block's window and change the values to –30 and 30. Do the same for the Enemies sprite. New clones will now have different colours!

Green and blue circles are friends.

Orange, yellow, pink, and purple circles are enemies.

when I start as a clone

set color ▼ effect to (pick random (–30) to (30))

set ghost ▼ effect to (50)

repeat (300)

Insert this instruction immediately after "when I start as a clone".

▷ **Change the size**

Add the "change size by" block to the scripts of both the Friends and Enemies sprites to make each clone a random size. Alter the scoring so that the size of the circle you touch determines how many points you score. You'll also need to change the totals needed to win or lose. Try more than 2000 points for victory, and less than –2000 for defeat.

From green Operators section

when I start as a clone

change size by (pick random (–30) to (30))

set ghost ▼ effect to (50)

repeat (300)

Change the values to "–30" and "30".

Change the Friends' score value to this.

change Score ▼ by (size)

change Score ▼ by ((0) – (size))

Use this scoring for Enemies.

The bigger the clone, the more points you win or lose.

◁ **Shape shifting**

Introduce another shape into the game. It could be a square that eats red circles, a triangle that runs away from the player, a hexagon that makes the player shrink or grow, or anything else you want to try.

Jumpy Monkey

How to build Jumpy Monkey

In the real world there are laws you just can't break. For example, the law of gravity means that something that goes up must always come down again. Jumpy Monkey shows you how to add gravity to your game worlds.

AIM OF THE GAME

The monkey is on a mission to collect bananas. Choose which direction he leaps in and how fast he goes. You need to send him over the palm tree to grab the bananas using the fewest possible jumps.

◁ **Launcher**
Point this arrow in the direction you want to launch the monkey by using the left and right arrow keys.

◁ **Monkey**
Select the monkey's launch speed with the up and down arrow keys, then press the space key to launch him.

◁ **Bananas**
If the monkey touches any of the bananas he will eat them. Keep going until he eats all the bananas.

The instructions appear on the game at the start.

Jumpy Monkey
by FunkyMonkey66 (unshared)

SET LAUNCH ANGLE ←→
SET LAUNCH SPEED ↑↓
PRESS SPACE TO FIRE

LaunchSpeed 11

The monkey is launched from the arrow when you press the space key.

This number shows you how fast the monkey will fly once he is launched.

The monkey flies
through the air
like a cannon ball.

GAME CONTROLS

Players use the arrow keys
and space key on the
keyboard as game controls.

Space

◁ **Flying monkey**
Try to collect all the
bananas using as few
launches as possible.
The game will record how
many launches you use.

There are three
bunches of bananas
to collect each time
you play the game.

Avoid the tree –
the monkey can't
fly through it.

Down with
gravity!

Launching the monkey

This game uses a big arrow to help the player choose the monkey's precise launch direction. We'll ignore gravity to start off with, but you'll need to add it later to get the monkey past the tree.

1 Start a new project and call it "Jumpy Monkey". Delete the cat sprite and load two sprites from the library – "Monkey2" and "Arrow1". Select the arrow sprite and rename it "Launcher" by clicking on the "i" and typing the new name into the box.

2 Go to Data, select "make a variable", and add a variable called "LaunchSpeed". The new variable will automatically show up on the stage.

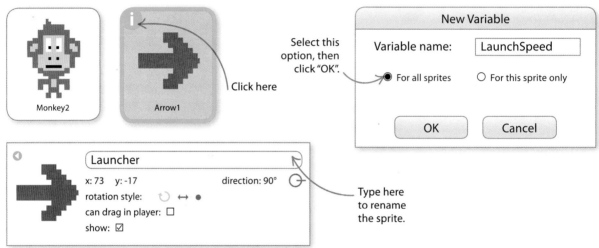

Monkey2

Arrow1

Click here

Select this option, then click "OK".

New Variable

Variable name: LaunchSpeed

◉ For all sprites   ○ For this sprite only

OK   Cancel

Launcher

x: 73   y: -17   direction: 90°

rotation style: ↻   ↔   •

can drag in player: ☐

show: ☑

Type here to rename the sprite.

3 Select the Launcher sprite, then add these three scripts to set up the Launcher and allow the player to control its angle using the left and right arrow keys on the keyboard. The direction of the arrow is the direction that he monkey will launch in. Run the scripts and try turning the arrow.

This block moves the arrow to the bottom left of the stage.

```
when       clicked
set  LaunchSpeed ▼  to  10
go to x: (-200) y: (-140)
point in direction  45 ▼
go to front
```

This keeps the arrow visible, with the monkey behind it.

This script runs when the left arrow key is pressed.

```
when  left arrow ▼  key pressed
turn ↺ ① degrees
```

This script runs when the right arrow key is pressed.

```
when  right arrow ▼  key pressed
turn ↻ ① degrees
```

4 Now that you can aim, you need controls to set the speed of the launch. Add these scripts to change the speed using the up and down arrow keys.

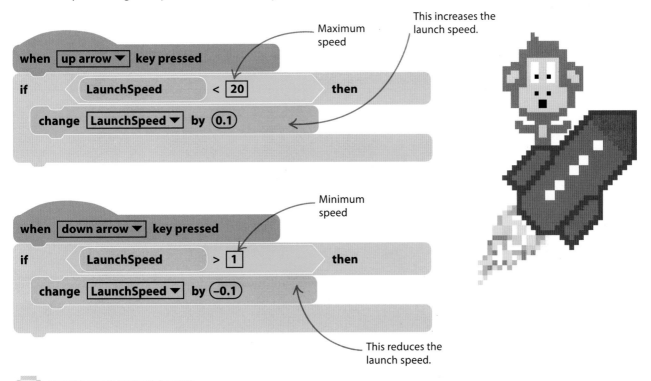

Maximum speed

This increases the launch speed.

when up arrow ▼ key pressed

if LaunchSpeed < 20 then

change LaunchSpeed ▼ by 0.1

Minimum speed

when down arrow ▼ key pressed

if LaunchSpeed > 1 then

change LaunchSpeed ▼ by -0.1

This reduces the launch speed.

▪▪▪ LINGO
Events

The key presses and mouse clicks that a computer detects are known as events. The brown Events blocks in Scratch trigger a script whenever a particular event occurs. We've seen them used with messages in Cheese Chase, but Scratch also lets you trigger scripts using keys, mouse clicks, sound levels, and even movement detected by a webcam. Don't be afraid to experiment.

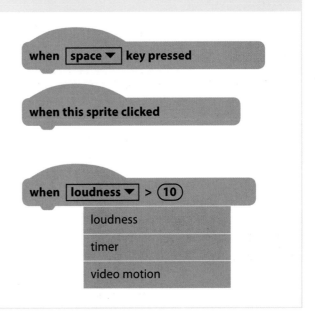

when space ▼ key pressed

when this sprite clicked

when loudness ▼ > 10

loudness

timer

video motion

▷ **Setting things off**
Events blocks such as these are used to trigger a script whenever the event they describe occurs.

5 Now select the Monkey sprite. Add this script to shrink him down to the right size and move him behind the Launcher.

when clicked
set size to (35) %
set rotation style don't rotate ▼
go to Launcher ▼

6 To launch the monkey when the space bar is pressed, add this new script to the Monkey sprite. "Repeat until" is a new type of loop block that keeps repeating the block inside until the condition becomes true – in this case, the monkey keeps moving until it touches the edge of the stage.

This makes the monkey's direction match the direction of the launch arrow.

when space ▼ key pressed
go to Launcher ▼
point in direction   direction ▼ of Launcher ▼
repeat until   touching edge ▼ ?
    move   LaunchSpeed   steps
go to Launcher ▼

The "repeat until" block keeps the monkey moving to the edge of the stage.

▪▪▪ **EXPERT TIPS**

"repeat until"

Do you want to keep repeating an action only until something happens and then get on with the rest of the script? The "repeat until" block can help your code when "forever" and "repeat" loops aren't flexible enough. Most programming languages use similar loops, but some call them "while" loops – these continue *while* the condition is true, rather than looping *until* the condition is true. There are always different ways to think about the same problem.

7 Try setting the Launcher angle and speed using the arrow keys, and pressing the space bar to fire the monkey. He goes in a completely straight line until he hits the edge of the stage. Real things don't do this – they fall back towards the ground as they move. We'll add gravity to the game later to make the monkey behave realistically.

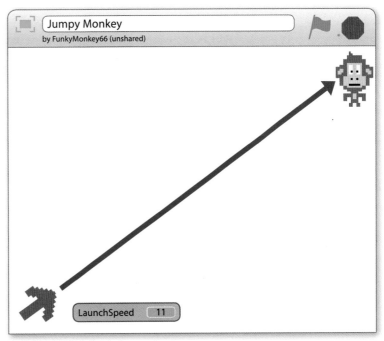

Jumpy Monkey
by FunkyMonkey66 (unshared)

LaunchSpeed   11

Bananas and palm trees

The point of this game is for the monkey to collect bananas. By using clones, you can add just one Bananas sprite but give the monkey plenty of fruit to aim for.

8 Add the Bananas sprite to the project. Make a variable for all sprites called "NumBananas" to keep track of the number of bananas on the stage – start with three. Build the following script to clone the bananas, but don't run it yet as you still need to tell the clones what to do.

```
when   clicked
hide
set  NumBananas ▼  to  3
repeat                NumBananas
  create clone of  myself ▼
```

We only need the clones, so hide the original Bananas sprite.

The loop runs three times.

9 Add the next script to place each banana clone in a random spot on the right of the stage, change how it looks, and make sure it's not hidden. The clone will wait for the monkey to touch it and then disappear. If it's the last banana, it sends a "GameOver" message, which you need to create as a new message.

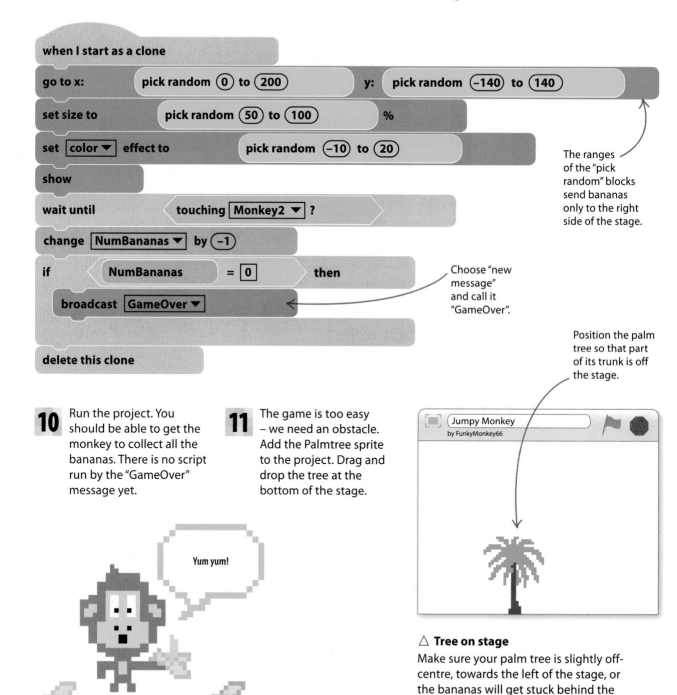

```
when I start as a clone

go to x:    pick random  0  to  200        y:    pick random  -140  to  140

set size to    pick random  50  to  100    %

set  color ▼  effect to    pick random  -10  to  20

show

wait until    touching  Monkey2 ▼  ?

change  NumBananas ▼  by  -1

if    NumBananas  =  0    then

    broadcast  GameOver ▼

delete this clone
```

The ranges of the "pick random" blocks send bananas only to the right side of the stage.

Choose "new message" and call it "GameOver".

Position the palm tree so that part of its trunk is off the stage.

10 Run the project. You should be able to get the monkey to collect all the bananas. There is no script run by the "GameOver" message yet.

11 The game is too easy – we need an obstacle. Add the Palmtree sprite to the project. Drag and drop the tree at the bottom of the stage.

Yum yum!

Jumpy Monkey
by FunkyMonkey66

△ **Tree on stage**
Make sure your palm tree is slightly off-centre, towards the left of the stage, or the bananas will get stuck behind the tree and the game won't work.

12 At the moment, the monkey can fly straight through the tree. Change his script so that he stops flying if he touches it.

The current script

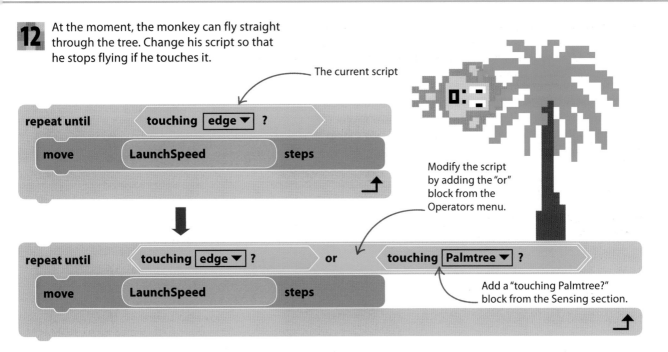

repeat until ⬡ touching [edge ▼] ?
move (LaunchSpeed) steps

Modify the script by adding the "or" block from the Operators menu.

repeat until ⬡ touching [edge ▼] ? ◇ or ◇ touching [Palmtree ▼] ?
move (LaunchSpeed) steps

Add a "touching Palmtree?" block from the Sensing section.

13 Run the project. The monkey should stop flying when he hits the tree, which makes any bananas to the right of the tree impossible to reach. Don't worry, gravity will come to the rescue soon.

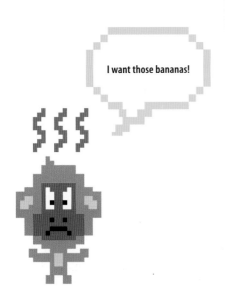

I want those bananas!

EXPERT TIPS

"or", "and", "not"

So far, most of the "if then" blocks in this book have tested only a single condition, such as "if touching cat" in the Star Hunter game. In this chapter, however, you need to test two conditions at once: "touching edge or touching Palmtree". Complex sets of condition like this occur a lot in coding, so you need a way to combine them. In Scratch, the green Operators blocks do the job. You'll see words like "or", "and", and "not" in almost every programming language, or special symbols that do the same job.

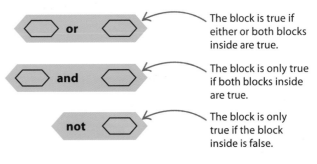

⬡ or ⬡ — The block is true if either or both blocks inside are true.

⬡ and ⬡ — The block is only true if both blocks inside are true.

not ⬡ — The block is only true if the block inside is false.

△ **Logic blocks**
Logical Operators blocks such as these three let you test for complex sets of conditions.

14 Make two more variables for all sprites: "FallSpeed" and "Gravity". Then add a "set Gravity" block to the monkey's "when clicked" script and amend his "when space key pressed" script as shown below. The new blocks use variables to simulate gravity. "FallSpeed" keeps track of how many steps the monkey needs to be moved down by gravity. The value of "Gravity" is how much "FallSpeed" increases by each time the monkey moves.

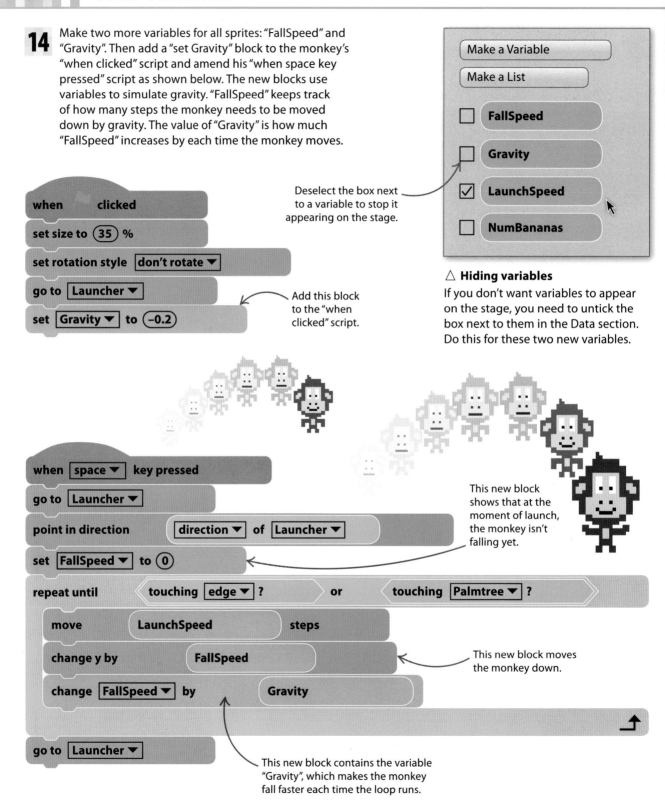

Make a Variable

Make a List

☐ **FallSpeed**

☐ **Gravity**

☑ **LaunchSpeed**

☐ **NumBananas**

Deselect the box next to a variable to stop it appearing on the stage.

△ **Hiding variables**

If you don't want variables to appear on the stage, you need to untick the box next to them in the Data section. Do this for these two new variables.

when clicked

set size to 35 %

set rotation style don't rotate ▾

go to Launcher ▾

set Gravity ▾ to -0.2

Add this block to the "when clicked" script.

when space ▾ key pressed

go to Launcher ▾

point in direction direction ▾ of Launcher ▾

set FallSpeed ▾ to 0

repeat until touching edge ▾ ? or touching Palmtree ▾ ?

move LaunchSpeed steps

change y by FallSpeed

change FallSpeed ▾ by Gravity

go to Launcher ▾

This new block shows that at the moment of launch, the monkey isn't falling yet.

This new block moves the monkey down.

This new block contains the variable "Gravity", which makes the monkey fall faster each time the loop runs.

Real world gravity

In the real world, when you try to throw something in a straight line it curves slowly back towards the ground as gravity pulls it down. To make the game work in the same way, you move the monkey along the straight line, but also add a downward move after each shift along that line, to create the same effect as the constant downward tug of gravity. This allows the monkey's movement to seem natural, making the game more engaging.

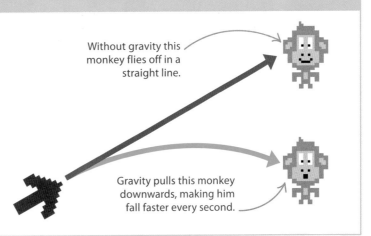

Without gravity this monkey flies off in a straight line.

Gravity pulls this monkey downwards, making him fall faster every second.

15 Run the project again – you can now direct the monkey over the tree to reach the tricky low bananas. But how exactly is the Scratch gravity working? Every second, the monkey falls a little bit faster than the second before, creating a downward curve.

◁ **Falling faster**
The "FallSpeed" variable makes the monkey fall further each time the "repeat" loop runs.

Falls this far in the first second.

Falls this far in the second second.

Falls this far in the third second.

Without gravity the monkey would get to here.

The monkey moves sideways by the same amount each second.

It falls by an increasing amount each second.

△ **Gravity effect**
When "FallSpeed" is combined with the straight line from the Launcher, the monkey's path curves back towards the ground in a realistic manner.

With gravity the monkey ends up here.

Game over

When the monkey has collected all the bananas, a "GameOver" message is broadcast, ending the game. Make a sign to go with it to tell the player how many launches they used to collect the bananas.

16 Click the paintbrush symbol ✐ to paint a new sprite and make a sign like the one below, leaving a gap in the text where the number of launches will go. You can make the sign as plain or as decorative as you like. Name the new sprite "Game Over".

WELL DONE!

You used   launches

Leave a gap here.

17 Now add a variable for all sprites to count the number of launches. Call this variable "Launches", show it on the stage, and right-click on it to change it to "large readout". This shows just the value and not the name of the variable. You'll reposition the launch counter later.

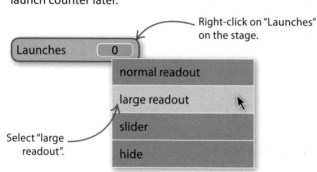

Right-click on "Launches" on the stage.

Launches   0

normal readout

large readout

slider

hide

Select "large readout".

18 Now add these scripts to your sign. Together, they will count the number of times you launch the monkey and will display that number at the end of the game.

```
when clicked
set Launches ▼ to 0
Hide variable Launches ▼
hide
```

You don't want to see this variable until the game's over.

```
when I receive GameOver ▼
go to x: 0 y: 0
go to front
show
Show variable Launches ▼
stop all ▼
```

This shows the value of "Launches" at the end of the game.

```
when space ▼ key pressed
change Launches ▼ by 1
```

This block counts the number of times the space key is pressed.

19 Run the game and collect all the bananas. When you see the "WELL DONE!" sign on the stage, drag the "Launches" counter into the gap in the sign. Scratch will remember its position in future games, so the sign will always be in the right place.

Drag the "Launches" number into the gap you left in the sign.

Jumpy Monkey
by FunkyMonkey66 (unshared)

7

WELL DONE!

You used   launches

20 To add a backdrop, click on the stage information area in the bottom left and then choose the Backdrop tab at the top. Either paint your own scenery or load an image from the library. Use the text tool to add the game's instructions to the image, as shown below.

Draw the arrows with the pencil or paintbrush tool.

Jumpy Monkey
by FunkyMonkey66 (unshared)

LAUNCH ANGLE ← →
LAUNCH SPEED ↑ ↓
PRESS SPACE TO FIRE

Make some noise

To make the game more interesting, you can add some sound effects. Follow the instructions below to play different sounds when the monkey is launched and when he eats the bananas.

21 Click the Monkey sprite, select the Sounds tab, and load "boing" from the library. Then add a "play sound" block to the existing monkey script in the position shown here. This will make the "boing" sound play every time the monkey jumps.

when [space ▼] key pressed

play sound [boing ▼]

go to [Launcher ▼]

Add this sound block to the existing Monkey2 script.

22 Click the Bananas sprite and load "chomp" from the sound library. Then add a "play sound" block to the existing banana script in the position shown here. Now the "chomping" sound will play each time the monkey gets a banana.

show

wait until [touching [Monkey2 ▼] ?]

play sound [chomp ▼]

change [NumBananas ▼] by (-1)

Add this sound block to the existing Bananas sprite script.

Playing with gravity

Add a slider to the game to allow you to experiment with the "Gravity" variable. The slider will allow you to tweak the "Gravity" value – you can even make the monkey fall upwards.

23 To adjust gravity in your game world, show the "Gravity" variable on the stage by ticking its box in the Data section. Then right-click the variable display on the stage and select "slider". The slider lets you change the value of a variable on the stage.

Select the "slider" option.

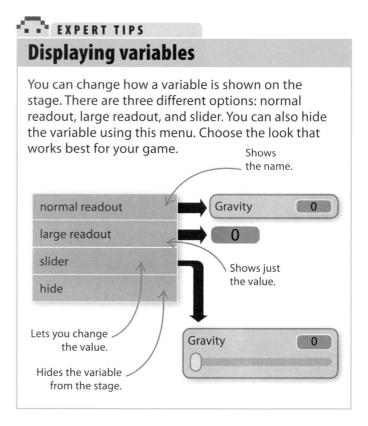

EXPERT TIPS
Displaying variables

You can change how a variable is shown on the stage. There are three different options: normal readout, large readout, and slider. You can also hide the variable using this menu. Choose the look that works best for your game.

Shows the name.

Shows just the value.

Lets you change the value.

Hides the variable from the stage.

24 To set the range of the variable, right-click on the slider and type in the minimum and maximum values – for this game use –2.0 and 2.0. Make sure you type 2.0 not just 2, or the slider will only allow you to select whole numbers within the range.

Set the range of the slider by right-clicking on the slider again.

Move this with your mouse to adjust the number.

25 Now play around with the gravity settings in this game using the slider. Using the suggested value of –0.2 works well, but have a look at what happens when you increase or decrease this number – if it is positive the monkey will fall upwards.

26 When you've finished experimenting with gravity, right-click on the slider and select "hide" to return the game to normal. Now you know how gravity works, you could try making a version of the game with reverse gravity so the monkey falls upwards. Think about what changes you'd need to make to the game for this to work, like moving the Launcher to fire downwards.

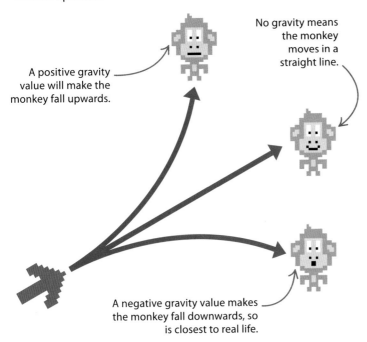

No gravity means the monkey moves in a straight line.

A positive gravity value will make the monkey fall upwards.

A negative gravity value makes the monkey fall downwards, so is closest to real life.

Help!!!

∙ ∙ ▌ GAME DESIGN

Game physics

Physics is the science of forces and movement in the real world. Game physics is all about getting that science into games, so that things react and move around in realistic ways – being pulled down by gravity, for instance, or bouncing. Programmers have to solve all sorts of physics problems to make games more realistic or fun. When objects collide, should they bounce or crunch? How should objects move when they go underwater or into space?

△ **Defying gravity**
Game physics doesn't have to be like real-world physics – you can create worlds with gravity that makes things fall upwards or even sideways. Gravity can be much stronger or weaker than in real life – perhaps balls fly higher with each bounce, until they shoot off into space.

Hacks and tweaks

Congratulations – you've built your first game with gravity. Once you've tried the game a few times, you can start to play around with the code to make the game your own. Here are a few ideas to try out.

◁ **Banana bonanza**
Try adding more bananas, making then bigger or smaller, and put them in different places on the screen.

▽ **Fruit salad**
Add more fruit with a different score for each type. You'll need to make a "Score" variable and add extra sprites – there are oranges and watermelons in the Scratch sprite library.

▽ **Beat the clock**
You can add a timer to make the player complete the game in a set time. Create a new variable called "TimeLeft" and add the script below to the Monkey2 sprite. Then create a new sprite, click on the Costumes tab, and make a sign that says "Times Up!" Finally, add the two scripts on the right to this sprite.

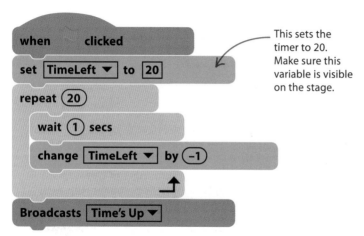

This sets the timer to 20. Make sure this variable is visible on the stage.

```
when  clicked
set TimeLeft ▼ to 20
repeat 20
    wait 1 secs
    change TimeLeft ▼ by -1
Broadcasts Time's Up ▼
```

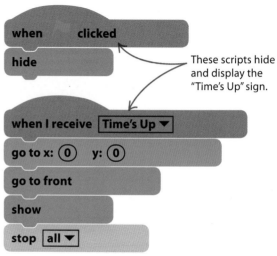

```
when  clicked
hide

when I receive Time's Up ▼
go to x: 0  y: 0
go to front
show
stop all ▼
```

These scripts hide and display the "Time's Up" sign.

▽ Mouse control

You could use a computer mouse as the controller for this game instead of the keyboard. The three blocks below allow you to set the launch angle and speed as well as making the monkey jump. See if you can figure out some code to use them.

Use this block to make the monkey jump.

`mouse down?`

`distance to  mouse-pointer ▼`

This block could be used to set launch speed.

`point towards  mouse-pointer ▼`

Use this block to set launch angle.

▷ Bouncing bananas

To make the game a bit harder, you could try changing the Bananas sprite scripts so that the bananas bounce up and down on the stage.

▷ Danger! Snake!

Add another challenge by creating an obstacle that gets in the monkey's way or maybe ends the game – perhaps a giant monkey-eating snake or spider?

▽ Bug or bonus?

You might have discovered that you can adjust the monkey's speed in flight with the arrow keys. You can fix this by adding a new variable, "MonkeySpeed", and copying the value of "LaunchSpeed" into it at launch. Then use MonkeySpeed not LaunchSpeed in the move block for the monkey. Or, if you enjoy being able to change the monkey's speed, leave the game as it is.

▽ Launch speed slide

You've already tried adding a slider to control gravity. You could also add a slider to adjust launch speed.

Sliders let you change these variables using the mouse instead of the arrow keys.

Doom on the Broom

How to build Doom on the Broom

Games usually have a theme. This spooky game starts with bats swooping in on the player, followed by scary ghouls and monsters. Get ready to bring these sprites to life with animation.

AIM OF THE GAME

The witch is out riding her broomstick in the woods when creatures of the night begin to advance on her from all sides. She must cast her fireball spell to dispose of the bats, ghosts, ghouls, and dragons that have taken a fancy to her for dinner.

◁ **Witch**
The witch sits in the centre of the screen. Spin her broomstick with the arrow keys and cast fireballs with the space bar.

◁ **Enemies**
Every enemy hit by a fireball is destroyed and a point is scored. As you win points, the game speeds up.

◁ **Lives**
The witch loses a life if she is touched by any of her enemies. But if a flying hippo touches her, she wins an extra life.

Slow-moving ghosts drift in and fade away when hit.

Doom on the Broom
by WorkingWitch111 (unshared)

Score   25

Superfast brown bats have a speedier attack.

Black bats flap straight towards the witch.

To make the game last longer, you can increase the number of lives.

GAME CONTROLS

Use the arrow keys and the space bar on the keyboard as game controls.

Space

Lives 3

Fireballs are the witch's only weapon.

Fire-breathing dragons spiral in to catch the witch.

◁ **Staying alive**

As the game progresses, more and more monsters fly towards the witch. The player must turn the broomstick quickly and pick off enemies one by one.

Do you dare to begin?

The witch stays in the centre of the stage.

Like dragons, ghouls spiral in towards the witch.

Setting the scene

Doom on the Broom has a spooky theme. The sprites, backdrop, and music are all chosen to create a certain atmosphere that draws the player into the game world. Start by putting together the Witch sprite, a dark wood, and some creepy music.

1 Start a new project and call it Doom on the Broom. Delete the Cat sprite. Click the sprite symbol 👹 in the sprites list and choose the Witch sprite from the library.

Click to open the sprite library.

The Witch sprite will appear in your sprites list.

Witch

2 Click on the "Choose backdrop from library" symbol 🏞 and add the backdrop "woods". This will lend an eerie setting to the game, which fits with the theme.

3 Load the sound "cave" from the sound library and add this script to the stage's scripts area. Run the project and admire the spooky atmosphere you've created.

This block keeps the sound playing in a loop.

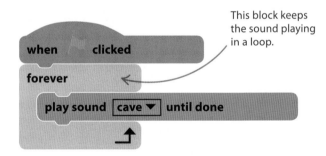

```
when [flag] clicked
forever
    play sound [cave ▼] until done
```

4 For extra creepiness, add another script to the stage to make it slowly but continually change colour while the game is playing.

This block changes all the colours in the backdrop by a small amount each time it's run.

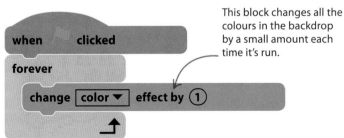

```
when [flag] clicked
forever
    change [color ▼] effect by (1)
```

5 Now add the witch's first enemy: a sinister black bat. Open the sprite library, select Bat2, and click "OK".

Bat2

6 The bat looks scary but it doesn't move. Click the Costumes tab and look in the middle – you'll notice the bat has two different costumes. These two costumes can be used to make the bat flap its wings.

New costume:

1
bat2-a
139x87

2
bat2-b
151x78

7 Add this script to the bat to make the costumes swap back and forth. Now run the project to see the bat flapping its wings.

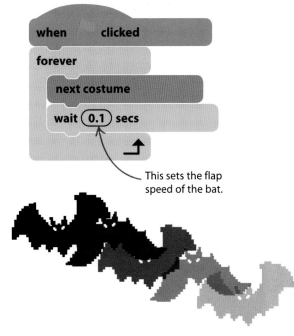

when ⚑ clicked

forever

next costume

wait (0.1) secs

This sets the flap speed of the bat.

GAME DESIGN

Animation

You can make pictures appear to move by showing slightly different versions of the same picture one after another. This fools the brain into thinking that it is a single moving image. This is called animation, and it is how all cartoons work. Scratch lets you animate a sprite by rapidly changing costumes that show it in different poses. When these costumes appear one after the other, you can see flapping bats, walking cats, and jumping frogs.

Controlling the witch

Your spooky game is now starting to take shape, but you'll need to add some more scripts to get things working. The next script lets the player take control of the witch.

8 Go to Data in the blocks palette and then click "Make a Variable". Create the variables "Score", "Lives", and "GameSpeed", making sure that the "For all sprites" option is selected. Show the variable "Score" and "Lives" on the stage. Add the following script to the witch to set things up and to control her with the arrow keys. Read the script carefully and test it to see if it works.

This block fixes the pace of the game at 1.

These blocks set up the game and the Witch sprite.

This control loop continually checks on the arrow keys that spin the witch.

This controls how fast the witch turns.

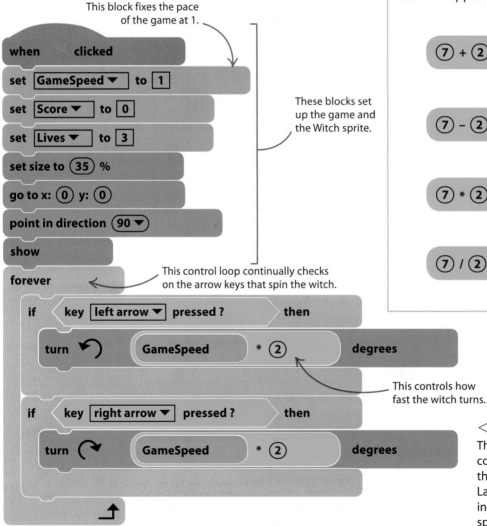

EXPERT TIPS

Arithmetic operators

Computer programmers have to use special symbols to do maths. Almost every computer language uses * for multiply and / for divide because the usual symbols aren't on a computer keyboard. Look in the green Operators section for the arithmetic operators. Click on the blocks in the scripts area to see the answers appear in a speech bubble.

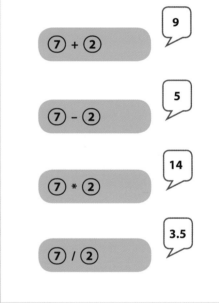

◁ **Controlling the pace**
The variable "GameSpeed" controls the overall pace of the game. For now fix it at 1. Later, you'll find out how to increase it as the score rises, speeding up the game.

Casting fireballs

The witch's only defence against the rampaging spooks will be her fireball spell. The next script will make a fireball shoot from her broomstick when the player presses the space bar.

9 Add the Ball sprite from the library and rename it "Fireball". It's currently too big, but you'll shrink it down in a moment.

Click the blue "i" button to open the information panel and rename the sprite.

Fireball

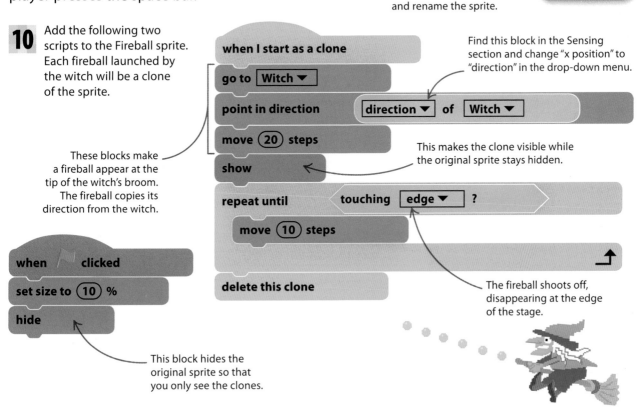

10 Add the following two scripts to the Fireball sprite. Each fireball launched by the witch will be a clone of the sprite.

```
when I start as a clone
go to  Witch ▼
point in direction    direction ▼  of  Witch ▼
move (20) steps
show
repeat until        touching  edge ▼  ?
    move (10) steps
delete this clone
```

Find this block in the Sensing section and change "x position" to "direction" in the drop-down menu.

These blocks make a fireball appear at the tip of the witch's broom. The fireball copies its direction from the witch.

This makes the clone visible while the original sprite stays hidden.

The fireball shoots off, disappearing at the edge of the stage.

```
when  clicked
set size to (10) %
hide
```

This block hides the original sprite so that you only see the clones.

```
when  clicked
forever
    if    key  space ▼  pressed ?    then
        create clone of  Fireball ▼
        wait until       not       key  space ▼  pressed ?
```

This block creates a clone and triggers the script above.

11 Now add this script to the witch to create a clone of the Fireball sprite when the space bar is pressed. The "wait until" block pauses the script until the space bar is released, so only one fireball is launched for each press. Try the script and check if you can spin the witch and shoot fireballs.

Without this block, the player could hold the space bar for a constant stream of fireballs.

Bat attack

One flapping bat isn't going to scare a powerful spellcaster like the witch, but you can add clones to make a whole squadron of bats.

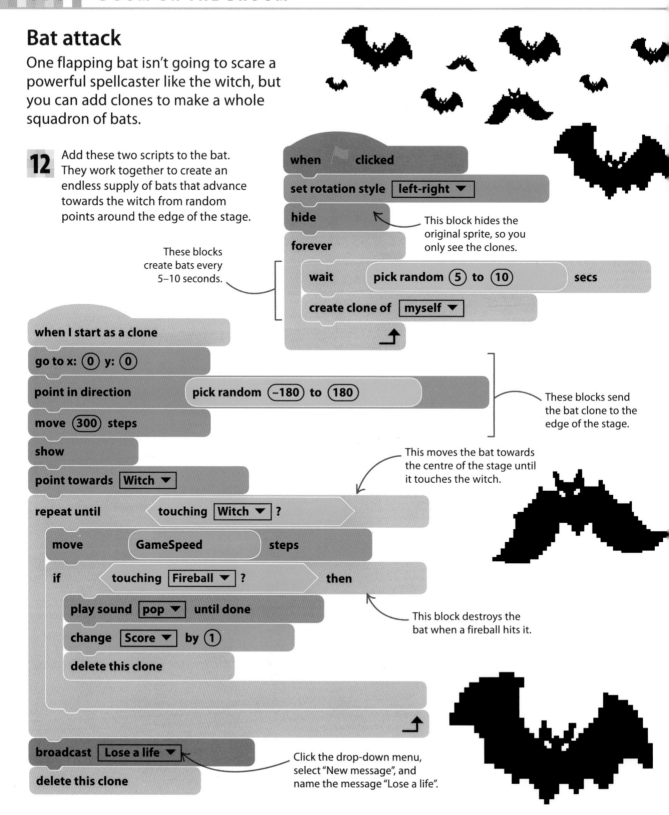

12 Add these two scripts to the bat. They work together to create an endless supply of bats that advance towards the witch from random points around the edge of the stage.

when ◢ clicked

set rotation style [left-right ▼]

hide

This block hides the original sprite, so you only see the clones.

forever

    wait (pick random (5) to (10)) secs

These blocks create bats every 5–10 seconds.

    create clone of [myself ▼]

when I start as a clone

go to x: (0) y: (0)

point in direction (pick random (−180) to (180))

move (300) steps

These blocks send the bat clone to the edge of the stage.

show

point towards [Witch ▼]

This moves the bat towards the centre of the stage until it touches the witch.

repeat until ⟨ touching [Witch ▼] ? ⟩

    move (GameSpeed) steps

    if ⟨ touching [Fireball ▼] ? ⟩ then

This block destroys the bat when a fireball hits it.

        play sound [pop ▼] until done

        change [Score ▼] by (1)

        delete this clone

broadcast [Lose a life ▼]

Click the drop-down menu, select "New message", and name the message "Lose a life".

delete this clone

▷ How does it work?

The three blue Motion blocks at the start of the bat clone's script move the clone to a random point at the edge of the stage. The hidden clone first moves to the centre and picks a random direction. Then it moves 300 steps – far enough to reach the edge in any direction. This way, bat clones will attack from every direction with equal chance. The witch doesn't touch the bat when it first moves to the centre, because you can't touch a hidden sprite.

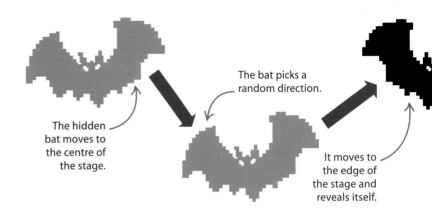

The bat picks a random direction.

The hidden bat moves to the centre of the stage.

It moves to the edge of the stage and reveals itself.

13 It's a good idea to remove all the bats whenever the witch loses a life. This gives her a chance to recover before the next wave of attackers. Add this script to the bat to do the job. When the message "Lose a life" is received, every clone runs the script and all the bats disappear.

14 Run the project to see if it works. A bat should appear after a few seconds and will move towards the witch. Soon more will appear. The witch should be able to use her fireballs to destroy them. All the bats will disappear when one finally reaches the witch.

```
when I receive  Lose a life ▼

delete this clone
```

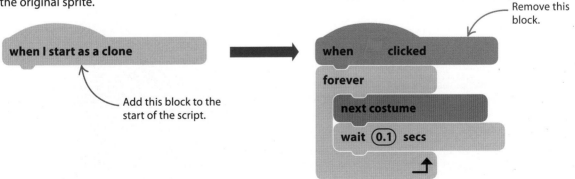

15 You might notice that the bats aren't flapping any more. To fix this, adjust the script below so that it runs for each clone rather than just the original sprite.

```
when I start as a clone
```

Add this block to the start of the script.

Remove this block.

```
when  clicked

forever
    next costume
    wait (0.1) secs
```

Adding explosions

Not much happens when the witch loses a life. Fix this to make the witch go out with a bang by creating some fireworks, adding a scream, and updating the counter that shows how many lives she has left.

16 Add this script to the witch to make her react to losing a life. If she still has lives left, she will disappear for two seconds before returning to battle. If she's out of lives, then it's game over. Add a new message, "GameOver", which you'll need later in the project. Now try the game again. The witch should lose lives and stop completely when the "Lives" variable has a value of 0.

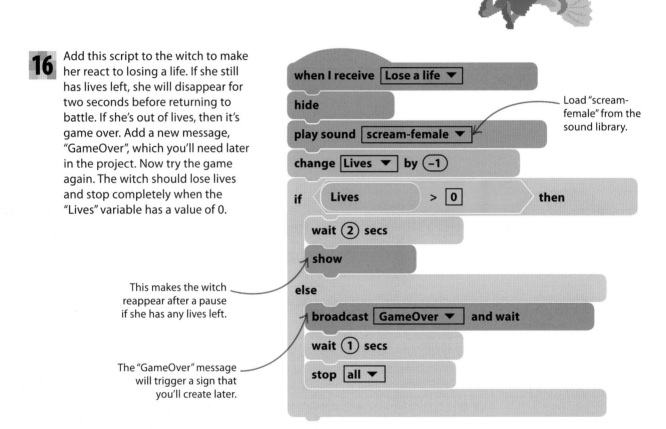

Load "scream-female" from the sound library.

This makes the witch reappear after a pause if she has any lives left.

The "GameOver" message will trigger a sign that you'll create later.

17 To create fireworks you need a new sprite. Load another Ball sprite from the sprite library rather than copying the Fireball sprite. Rename this new sprite "Explosion" and then click on the Costumes tab. Select the second costume so that the ball turns blue.

Select the second costume for the Ball sprite.

18 Now add these two scripts to the Explosion sprite. The first script creates 72 tiny, hidden blue ball clones, all pointing in different directions. The second script makes them fly out in a circle from the witch's location. Read the scripts carefully and try to work out what triggers the explosion.

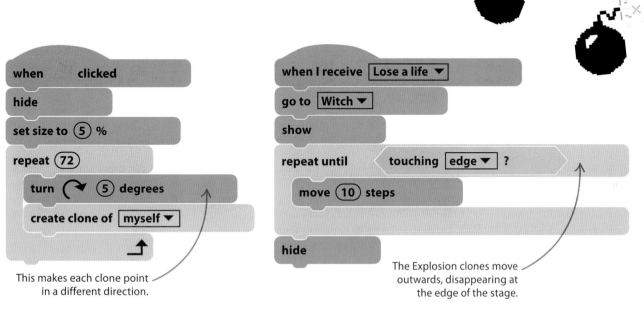

```
when [flag] clicked
hide
set size to (5) %
repeat (72)
    turn ↻ (5) degrees
    create clone of [myself ▼]
    ↱
```

This makes each clone point in a different direction.

```
when I receive [Lose a life ▼]
go to [Witch ▼]
show
repeat until < touching [edge ▼] ? >
    move (10) steps
hide
```

The Explosion clones move outwards, disappearing at the edge of the stage.

19 When the Explosion sprite receives the message "Lose a life", all the blue ball clones appear at the witch's location and explode out to the edge of the stage before hiding once again. Run the game and let a bat reach the witch to check how it works.

Doom on the Broom
by WorkingWitch111 (unshared)

Score 0   Lives 1

When a bat touches the witch, she explodes into a circle of flying blue balls.

Speedy spectre

It's now time to increase the fear factor and add a different type of bat to the game. You can copy the existing black bat, and add new costumes and alter the scripts to create a superfast brown bat.

20 To avoid having to rebuild every script from the black bat, simply right-click it and create a copy by selecting "duplicate". A sprite named Bat3 will appear in the sprites list. Rename it "Fast bat".

info

duplicate

Click here to copy the sprite.

Bat 2

21 Click on Fast bat's Costumes tab – you'll see the copied black bat's two costumes. To make Fast bat look different from the black bat, you need to load some new costumes. Click on the symbol ♣ at the top to choose a new costume from the library.

Scripts   Costumes

New costume:

Click here to add new costumes.

1

Bat2-a
139x87

2

Bat2-b
151x78

Use costumes to change our looks, expressions, or posture.

22 Add the two new costumes, "bat1-a" and "bat1-b". They show a brown bat with wings in two different positions.

3

bat1-a
115x125

4

bat1-b
101x103

23 Now delete the unnecessary black bat costumes in this sprite. To do this, select the costume you want to delete and then click the small "x" in the top right.

1

Click here to delete the costume.

Bat2-a
139x87

24 To speed up the fast bat, change its "move" block to make the brown bat move twice as fast as the black bat.

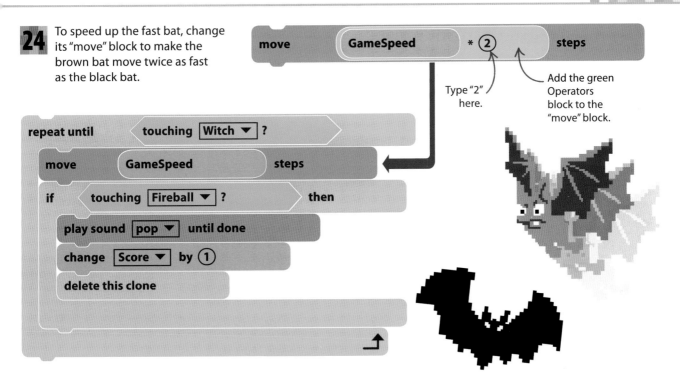

move (GameSpeed * 2) steps

Type "2" here.

Add the green Operators block to the "move" block.

repeat until (touching Witch ▼ ?)
  move (GameSpeed) steps
  if (touching Fireball ▼ ?) then
    play sound pop ▼ until done
    change Score ▼ by 1
    delete this clone

25 The game would be too hard with lots of fast bats, so make the following changes to the existing script to make them appear later in the game and less frequently.

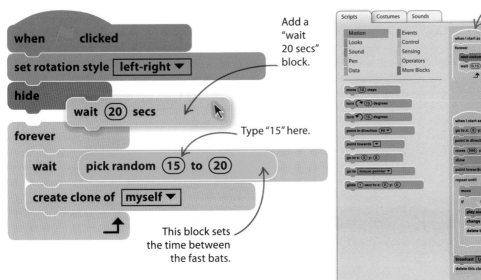

when [flag] clicked
set rotation style left-right ▼
hide
wait 20 secs
forever
  wait pick random 15 to 20
  create clone of myself ▼

Add a "wait 20 secs" block.

Type "15" here.

This block sets the time between the fast bats.

26 Check you have four scripts in Fast bat's scripts area, just like in Bat2. Run the game. After a few black bats have attacked, a faster, much more dangerous one will appear, flapping away.

Fast bat's scripts area should look like this.

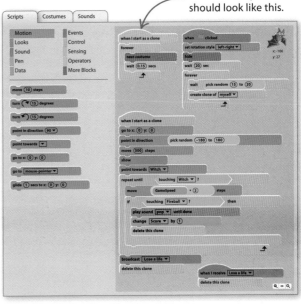

Fire-breathing dragon

The witch's next enemy is a fire-breathing dragon. Instead of flapping straight towards the witch as the bats do, it will spiral in slowly, giving her more time to defend herself.

27 Copy the Bat2 sprite again, but rename it "Dragon". Load the two new costumes "dragon1-a" and "dragon1-b", then delete the two bat costumes.

Dragon

Type the new sprite's name here.

Dragon

x: -127   y: 106   direction: 90°
rotation style: ↻ ↔ ●
can drag in player: ☐
show: ☑

28 Now make a few changes to the scripts in the copied sprite. First, change the costume script to make the dragon breathe fire in short bursts.

when I start as a clone

forever
  switch costume to dragon1-a ▼
  wait 2 secs
  switch costume to dragon1-b ▼
  wait 0.5 secs

The first costume shows the dragon with no fire.

The second costume shows the dragon breathing fire.

29 Next, modify the dragon's movement to make it fly in a spiral path by moving the "point towards Witch" block into the "repeat until" loop and adding a "turn right 80 degrees" block.

repeat until ⟨ touching Witch ▼ ? ⟩
  point towards Witch ▼
  turn ↻ 80 degrees
  move GameSpeed steps
  if ⟨ touching Fireball ▼ ? ⟩ then
    play sound pop ▼ until done
    change Score ▼ by 1
    delete this clone

These blocks make the dragon spiral in towards the witch.

30 Add a "wait 10 secs" block to the main script to delay the dragon's arrival on the stage. Then change the numbers in the "pick random" block to "10" and "15". This will make a clone of the dragon appear every 10–15 seconds. Once you've made all the changes, test the game to see if it works.

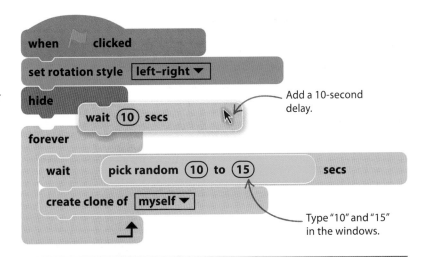

Add a 10-second delay.

Type "10" and "15" in the windows.

• • **GAME DESIGN**

Working with themes

In Doom on the Broom, spooky scenery and supernatural characters work together to give the game a theme. A strong theme that ties together the elements of a game can make it feel polished and professional. Working with themes is also great fun as you can let your imagination run wild.

△ Story
A background story or quest helps give a game a theme. Perhaps the player is trying to escape a haunted house, search for underwater treasure, or explore an alien planet. Instead of inventing a story, you can use a well-known one, but give it a twist, such as putting Goldilocks and the three bears in space.

△ Music and sound effects
Sounds in a game have a big influence on how the player feels. Spooky music makes the player nervous, but jolly music makes a game feel cheerful, even if the pictures are spooky. Choose sound effects carefully so they match the sprite or situation that triggers them.

△ Scenery
If you choose the right backdrop, sprites in the game will look like they are really there rather than stuck on top. You can create your own backdrops in Scratch's paint editor, but you can also upload images you've found or created elsewhere.

△ Sprites
The player is usually the hero in a game, so choose a likable sprite. The enemies don't have to look scary – even cute sprites can seem scary when they attack. If players have to collect objects, make them look valuable, such as coins or gems.

Ghost

Supernatural heroes should have supernatural enemies, so add some ghosts and ghouls to chase the witch. Instead of vanishing when fireballs hit them, the ghosts will fade away.

31 To create the ghost, make a copy of the Bat2 sprite again. Rename the new sprite "Ghost" and replace the Bat2 costumes with "ghost2-a" and "ghost2-b".

1
Bat2-a
139x87

2
ghost2-b
138x141

32 Modify the script below so the costumes change every second.

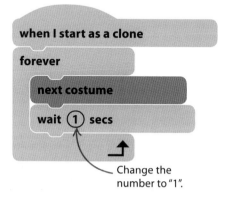

when I start as a clone
forever
    next costume
    wait 1 secs

Change the number to "1".

33 Change the ghost's script so that it moves slowly and fades out when hit by a fireball. Click the Sounds tab above the blocks palette and load the "screech" sound from the sound library. Then change the selection in the "play sound" block to "screech" to make the ghost scream when it vanishes.

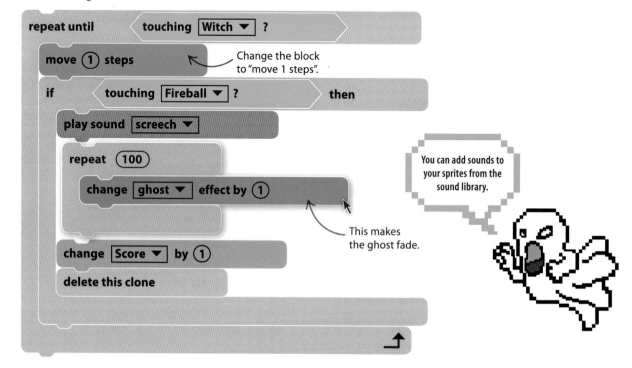

repeat until   touching Witch ?
    move 1 steps

Change the block to "move 1 steps".

    if   touching Fireball ?   then
        play sound screech
        repeat 100
            change ghost effect by 1

This makes the ghost fade.

        change Score by 1
        delete this clone

You can add sounds to your sprites from the sound library.

34 Now add a "wait 10 secs" block to the main script to delay the ghost's first appearance. Change the numbers in the "pick random" block to make ghosts appear more often than bats.

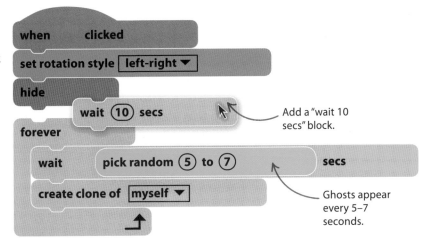

Add a "wait 10 secs" block.

Ghosts appear every 5–7 seconds.

35 Once all of your changes are complete, test the game. Try fireballing each enemy to make sure the code works.

The ghost should slowly fade when hit with a fireball.

36 The Scratch library has two ghoul costumes that you can use to make another animated enemy. Copy the Dragon sprite and rename the copy "Ghoul". Click the Costumes tab, load the two ghoul costumes – "ghoul-a" and "ghoul-b" – and then delete the dragon's costumes. Update the ghoul's script to use the new costumes and adjust the timings.

Double-click on the header block to see the animation working in the sprites list.

ghoul-a   ghoul-b

Finishing touches

It's time to add some finishing touches to the game. To make it look more professional, add a game-over screen that appears when the witch runs out of lives. You can also program the witch to give instructions to the players at the start of the game.

37 Click on the paintbrush symbol / in the sprites list to create a new sprite in the paint editor. Using "Bitmap Mode", draw a rectangle and fill it with a dark colour. Now switch to "Vector Mode". Click on the text tool, choose a font you like, and select red for the text colour. Click in the rectangle and type "GAME OVER!" and use the selection tool to make the text large. Remember to fix the centre of the sprite with the "Set costume centre" tool.

Type "GAME OVER!" here.

"Set costume centre" tool

Selection tool

Select a font here.

38 Now add these scripts to the new sprite to hide it at the start and show it only at the end when the witch loses all her lives. Run the game. Once the witch loses all her lives, the message will be displayed on the stage.

Rename the sprite "Game Over".

Game Over

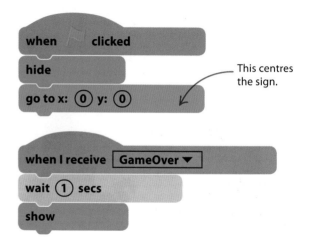

```
when [flag] clicked
hide
go to x: (0) y: (0)
```

This centres the sign.

```
when I receive GameOver ▼
wait (1) secs
show
```

39 Add a script to the witch so that she gives instructions to the player at the start of the game. You can change the three seconds in the "say" block if it's too quick, but not for too long – those bats won't wait.

Press arrow keys to turn. Press space bar to cast a fireball.

```
when [ clicked
say [ Press arrow keys to turn. Press space bar to cast a fireball. ▼ ] for (3) secs
```

Type the instructions here.

Challenger mode

As players become more skilled and score more points, they may start to get bored with the game. You can prevent this by making the game faster as it progresses.

40 To make the game speed up as the player scores points, add a block inside the witch's movement loop that sets the "GameSpeed" variable using the variable "Score".

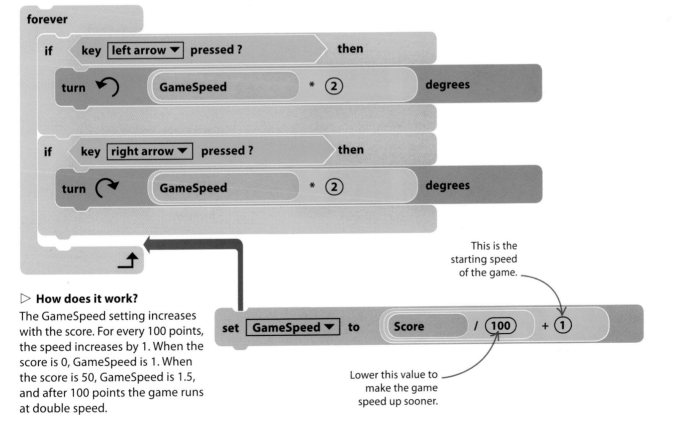

```
forever
  if < key [ left arrow ▼ ] pressed ? > then
    turn ↺ ( GameSpeed * (2) ) degrees
  if < key [ right arrow ▼ ] pressed ? > then
    turn ↻ ( GameSpeed * (2) ) degrees
```

This is the starting speed of the game.

```
set [ GameSpeed ▼ ] to ( ( Score / (100) ) + (1) )
```

Lower this value to make the game speed up sooner.

▷ **How does it work?**
The GameSpeed setting increases with the score. For every 100 points, the speed increases by 1. When the score is 0, GameSpeed is 1. When the score is 50, GameSpeed is 1.5, and after 100 points the game runs at double speed.

Extra lives hippo

So far you've mainly added enemies. To help the player, add a friendly flying hippo that gives the witch extra lives if it reaches her without getting hit by a fireball.

41 Copy the Bat2 sprite, but replace its costumes with two copies of hippo1. Use the paint editor to write the messages "EXTRA LIFE" and "DON'T FIREBALL ME!" on the costumes so the player knows it isn't an enemy. Rename the sprite "Hippo".

42 Amend the scripts so that instead of gaining a point when you fireball the hippo, you earn an extra life when it touches you. Change the value in the "point in direction" block so the text on the hippo doesn't get reversed.

Change this value to "0".

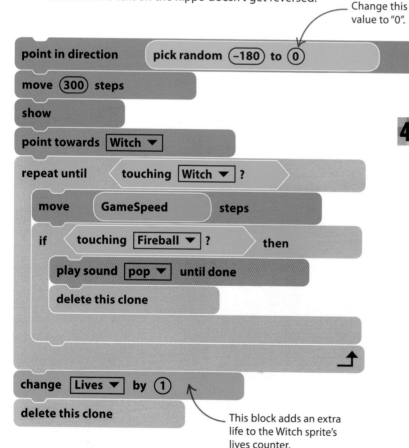

This block adds an extra life to the Witch sprite's lives counter.

43 Change the wait time in the costume script so that the hippo swaps costumes once a second, giving players time to read the signs.

This makes the hippo alternate between its two costumes every second.

44 To avoid making the game too easy, make the extra lives hippos rare. Change this script so they appear only every 30–60 seconds.

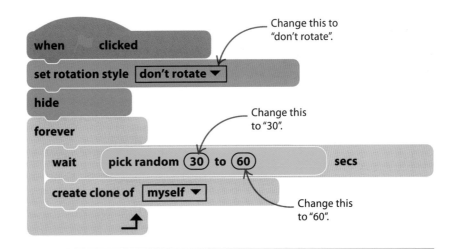

Change this to "don't rotate".

when [clicked]
set rotation style [don't rotate ▼]
hide
forever
    wait [pick random (30) to (60)] secs
    create clone of [myself ▼]

Change this to "30".

Change this to "60".

Hacks and tweaks

Now that you've got your game to work, you can experiment and make it your own by changing and adding elements. Try these suggestions to get started.

▷ **Flying Witch**
You can make the witch fly instead of rotating on the spot by adding the script shown here. To make her turn faster while flying, increase the numbers in her "turn" blocks.

when [clicked]
forever
    move (1) steps

This block will keep the witch flying.

△ **Spell binder**
Can you think of another spell that the witch can cast? Tweak her script and costumes so she strikes her enemies with lightning, or make her cast some other fancy spells.

▷ **Mouse control**
Use this script to let the player spin the witch with a mouse rather than the keyboard. If the game is too easy, increase the GameSpeed value. You can also try changing the code so the computer mouse casts the fireballs.

when [clicked]
forever
    point towards [mouse-pointer ▼]
    turn ↻ (45) degrees

This block stops the controls from being too easy.

Dog's Dinner

How to build Dog's Dinner

Dog's Dinner is a platform game. In this type of game, the player's character jumps from platform to platform collecting goodies and avoiding enemies and traps. The key to success is timing your jumps perfectly so you stay in the game.

AIM OF THE GAME

The dog likes bones but hates junk food. Steer him through three levels, jumping from platform to platform. Collect all the tasty bones on the stage and then go through the portal to the next level. But make sure he avoids the unhealthy cakes, cheesy-puffs, and donuts!

◁ **Dog**
Use the left and right arrow keys to make the dog run. When he needs to jump, press the space key.

◁ **Bones**
You need to collect all the bones to open the portal to the next level. It will remain shut until you've got them all.

◁ **Junk food**
If the dog touches any junk food, it's game over and you have to start again on Level 1 – no matter which level you were on!

The dog runs and jumps around the level. He can jump only when he's standing on a platform.

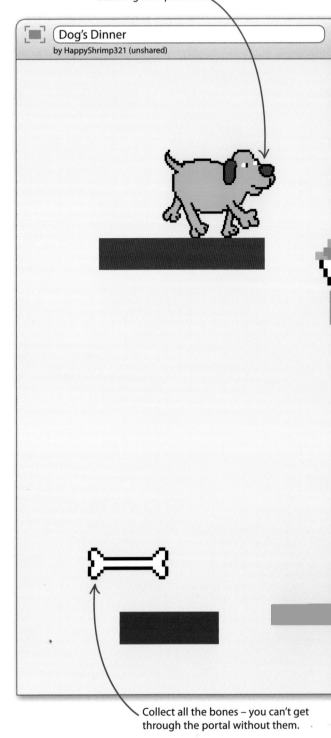

Dog's Dinner
by HappyShrimp321 (unshared)

Collect all the bones – you can't get through the portal without them.

Cheesy-puffs and cakes are static junk foods – unlike the donut, they don't move.

Click the green flag to start a new game.

Click the stop sign to end a game.

GAME CONTROLS

Players use the arrow keys and space bar on the keyboard as game controls.

The donut is a moving hazard. It flies from side to side, getting in the dog's way.

When you've collected all the bones, the portal to the next level flashes to show it's open.

I always demand quality food!

The dog must jump over the gaps.

Player on a platform

This is a complicated game, so you'll need to check your work carefully at every stage. But don't worry, the project builds gradually, one step at a time. Start by getting a very simple player sprite to work properly with a platform. At first, the player is just a red square. This makes it easy to sense collisions with the platforms. You can add the blue dog on top of it later.

At last! I'm going to be a star!

1 Create a new project and name it "Dog's Dinner". To make your simple player, click the paintbrush symbol at the top of the sprites list. Make sure you're in "Bitmap Mode". Choose red in the colour palette in the paint editor, select the rectangle tool, and click on the filled square option.

Click the paintbrush symbol.

New sprite:

Click on the filled square.

Choose red from the palette.

Select "Bitmap Mode".

100%

Bitmap Mode

Convert to vector

2 Hold down the shift key and drag the mouse-pointer over the paint editor to draw a small red square. If you click outside your block and look at the list of costumes, you'll see the size of the square; aim for 35x35.

The block should be smaller than the cat's face on the stage.

Scripts   Costumes

New costume:

costume1

2

costume1
35x35

When you click outside the block, its size is shown here.

3 You can resize your block if it's too big or too small. Using the "Select" tool, click and drag to draw a square around the block. Use the corner points to resize it. Do this until the size is right.

"Select" tool

Use the corner points to resize the block.

4 Select the "Set costume centre" tool in the top-right corner of the paint editor. Set the centre of your sprite near the top of the block (this will be useful later).

We don't need you for this game Cat, so we're deleting you.

Yes, I know... but I'll be back!

5 Rename the sprite "PlayerBlock". That's your player sprite done. Now you can delete the cat sprite.

PlayerBlock

6 Now add a simple platform. Click the paintbrush symbol in the sprites list again to create a new sprite. Use the rectangle tool to draw a floor with two obstacle blocks on top. Call this sprite "Platforms". On the stage, drag your PlayerBlock and place it between the obstacles, but make sure it's not touching the platform.

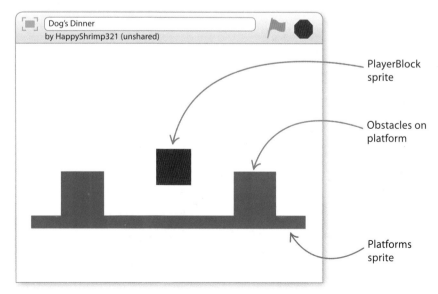

Dog's Dinner
by HappyShrimp321 (unshared)

PlayerBlock sprite

Obstacles on platform

Platforms sprite

Running around

The next step is to make the PlayerBlock run when the player presses the arrow keys. You'll need a script that will stop it running through obstacles by making it reverse when it touches them. To make the code easier to read, you'll be making your own customized Scratch blocks.

8 There are no blocks in this section yet, only some buttons. Click on the "Make a block" button, and a box called "New Block" will pop up. Type "Run controls" in the window to name your new block and then click "OK".

Type the name of your new block here.

7 With the PlayerBlock sprite selected, go to the blocks palette under the Scripts tab and click on More Blocks.

9 The new block appears in the More Blocks section, and a special purple "define" header block appears in the scripts area.

Subprograms

Scratch lets you group together blocks under a "define" header block and run them by using a new block that you name. This saves you building the same group of blocks again if you want to use it in more than one place. (However, the new block will only work with the sprite that you created it for.) Giving your new block a meaningful name will make your code easy to understand. Most programming languages let you take some useful code, give it a name, and wrap it up as a unit. Different languages call these units different things: subprograms, subroutines, procedures, and functions are some common names.

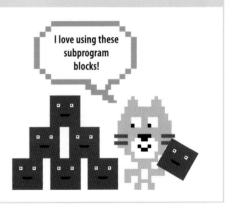

I love using these subprogram blocks!

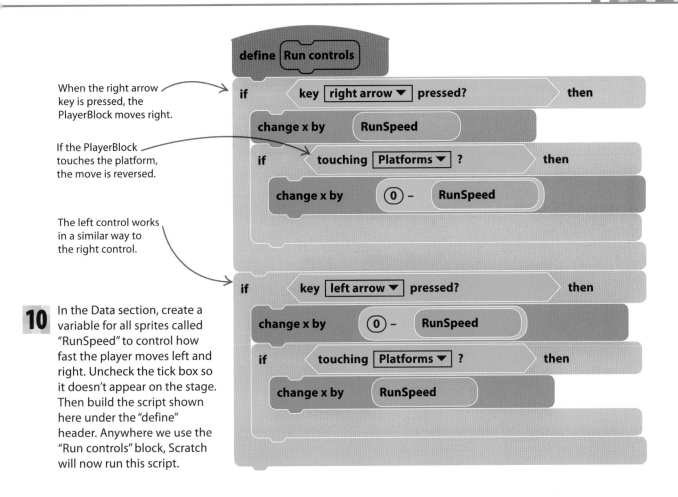

define **Run controls**

if ⟨ key [right arrow ▼] pressed? ⟩ then

   change x by   RunSpeed

   if ⟨ touching [Platforms ▼] ? ⟩ then

      change x by   ⟨ 0 ⟩ – RunSpeed

if ⟨ key [left arrow ▼] pressed? ⟩ then

   change x by   ⟨ 0 ⟩ – RunSpeed

   if ⟨ touching [Platforms ▼] ? ⟩ then

      change x by   RunSpeed

When the right arrow key is pressed, the PlayerBlock moves right.

If the PlayerBlock touches the platform, the move is reversed.

The left control works in a similar way to the right control.

10 In the Data section, create a variable for all sprites called "RunSpeed" to control how fast the player moves left and right. Uncheck the tick box so it doesn't appear on the stage. Then build the script shown here under the "define" header. Anywhere we use the "Run controls" block, Scratch will now run this script.

11 Next, add the script below to use your new custom block in a "forever" loop.

Type "5" here.

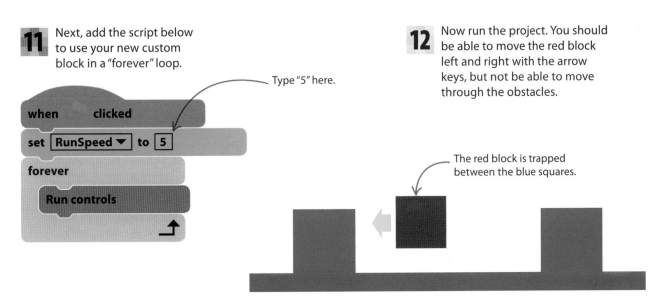

when ⚑ clicked

set [RunSpeed ▼] to ⟨ 5 ⟩

forever

   Run controls

12 Now run the project. You should be able to move the red block left and right with the arrow keys, but not be able to move through the obstacles.

The red block is trapped between the blue squares.

Up and down

Platform games are all about jumping. You can't jump without gravity, so you need to add some simulated gravity to the game. You might recognize how the simulated gravity works if you built the Jumpy Monkey game.

13 Add two more variables for all sprites: "Gravity" and "FallSpeed". Uncheck both tick boxes. Then click on More Blocks and make a new block called "Simulate gravity", following the script shown here. It moves the PlayerBlock down by the amount "FallSpeed" and then checks to see if the PlayerBlock has hit the platforms. If so, it reverses the last move and sets "FallSpeed" to zero so that the platform stops the player's fall.

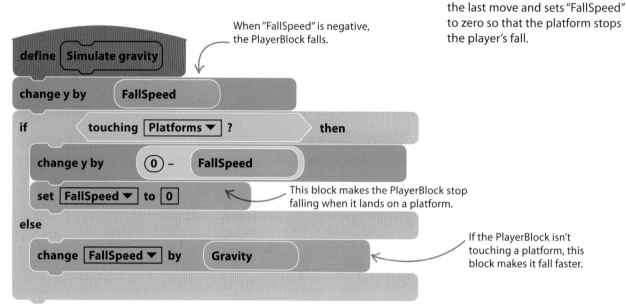

When "FallSpeed" is negative, the PlayerBlock falls.

This block makes the PlayerBlock stop falling when it lands on a platform.

If the PlayerBlock isn't touching a platform, this block makes it fall faster.

You need to set the value of gravity!

14 Insert the blocks shown here into the PlayerBlock's main script. Make sure you set the value of "Gravity" to "–1" and set FallSpeed to "0".

Insert "set Gravity to" and "set Fallspeed to" here.

Put "Simulate gravity" into the "forever" loop.

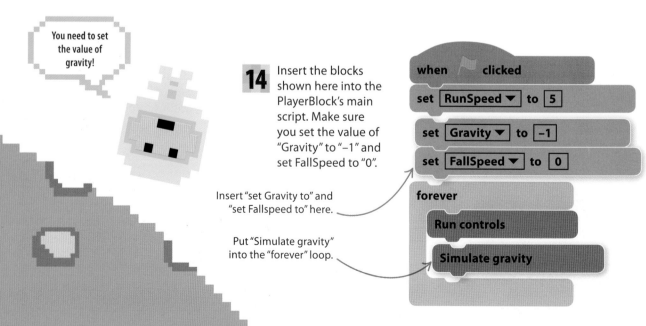

15 Run the project. Grab the red square with the mouse and drop it from above the platform. It will fall down and come to rest on the platform. But there's a problem: it slows down just above the platform. That's because our method makes the block reverse after hitting the platform and then start falling again at a slower speed. We can fix that later.

The PlayerBlock doesn't fall very smoothly as it gets near to the platform.

It finally stops one step above the platform.

16 Now to create the jump. It's really easy: just add some new code to give the PlayerBlock an upwards kick when you press the space bar. First, make a new variable for all sprites called "TakeoffSpeed". This is the player's upward speed on a jump. Then create a new block called "Jump control" and define it as shown here.

This block makes "FallSpeed" positive, so the PlayerBlock rises.

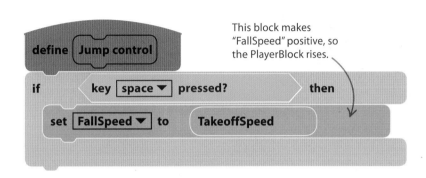

```
define  Jump control

if        key  space ▼  pressed?        then
    set  FallSpeed ▼  to    TakeoffSpeed
```

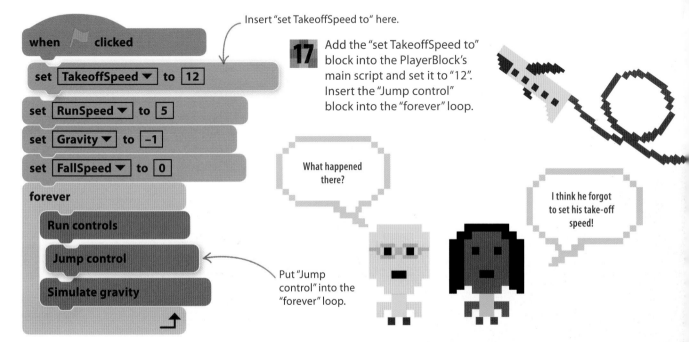

Insert "set TakeoffSpeed to" here.

```
when      clicked
    set  TakeoffSpeed ▼  to  12
set  RunSpeed ▼  to  5
set  Gravity ▼  to  –1
set  FallSpeed ▼  to  0
forever
    Run controls
    Jump control
    Simulate gravity
```

Put "Jump control" into the "forever" loop.

17 Add the "set TakeoffSpeed to" block into the PlayerBlock's main script and set it to "12". Insert the "Jump control" block into the "forever" loop.

What happened there?

I think he forgot to set his take-off speed!

18 Now run the project. Press the space key briefly. The PlayerBlock jumps up and comes back down again. You should be able to combine the run and jump controls to jump onto or over the obstacles on the platform. You now have the makings of a platform game! However, there's another bug: if you keep the space key pressed, the PlayerBlock goes up forever.

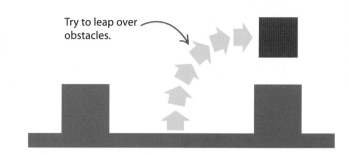

Try to leap over obstacles.

Fixing the jumping bugs

There are two bugs that spoil our jumps: one causes the PlayerBlock to jump infinitely high; the other stops it falling smoothly. You can fix them by tweaking the jump and gravity controls.

19 To fix the infinite jump bug, add a test to the "Jump control" script to check whether the player is on or just above the platform. (Remember that the "Simulate gravity" script leaves the PlayerBlock one step above the platform, so the two sprites aren't touching.) This fix will disable the space key when the player is in mid-jump.

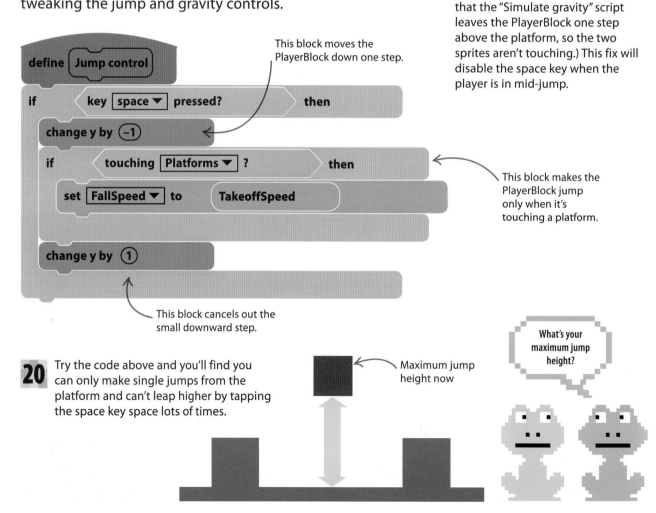

This block moves the PlayerBlock down one step.

This block makes the PlayerBlock jump only when it's touching a platform.

This block cancels out the small downward step.

20 Try the code above and you'll find you can only make single jumps from the platform and can't leap higher by tapping the space key space lots of times.

Maximum jump height now

What's your maximum jump height?

21 To fix the other jumping bug (pausing just above the platform and then falling slowly again), you need to change what happens when the PlayerBlock touches the platform. At the moment, the red square reverses by the whole "FallSpeed" number when it hits a platform. Instead, we'll make it reverse in tiny steps until it's just above the platform. Create a new variable called "ReverseStep" for all sprites. Change the "define Simulate gravity" script as shown here.

This "if then else" block works out which way the PlayerBlock needs to reverse.

If the PlayerBlock is falling ("FallSpeed" is negative), "ReverseStep" is set to +1 (up).

If the PlayerBlock is rising or stationary, "ReverseStep" is set to –1 (down).

The red square reverses by 1 step.

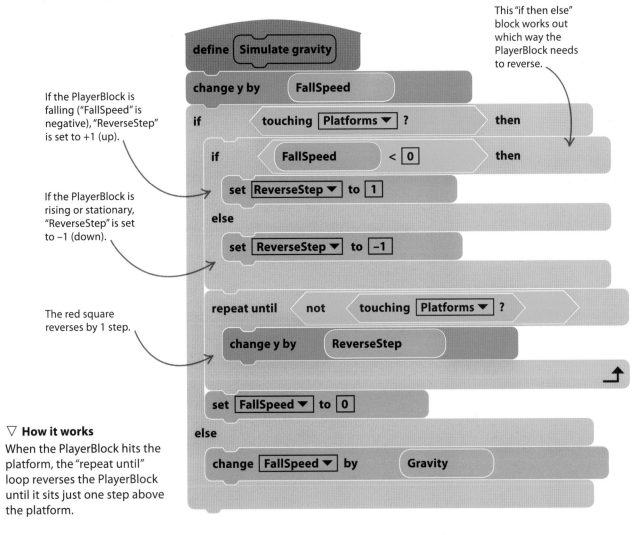

▽ **How it works**
When the PlayerBlock hits the platform, the "repeat until" loop reverses the PlayerBlock until it sits just one step above the platform.

The PlayerBlock lands inside the platform.

It reverses in single steps until it's just above the platform.

22 Try the jump again to see for yourself. You'll notice that the PlayerBlock rises back out of the platform very slowly. But we don't want that part to happen in slow motion! Scratch has a trick to fix this. Right-click on the "define Simulate gravity" header block and select "edit" from the pop-up menu that appears.

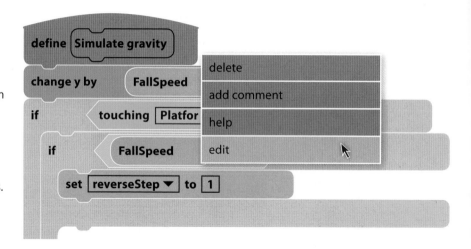

23 An "Edit Block" box appears. Click on "Options" and tick "Run without screen refresh". This will make the gravity script run all in one go (without showing each reverse step), which will get rid of the slow-motion effect.

Tick this box and the whole script will run much faster.

24 Now try jumping again. The tweaks you've made should help the PlayerBlock to jump and land very smoothly.

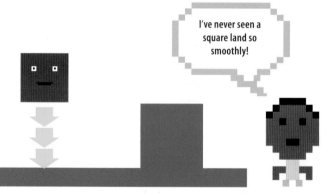

I've never seen a square land so smoothly!

· · **GAME DESIGN**

Which jump?

Games use many different types of jump. Which type you choose is key to your game's design. Here are three common jumps.

▽ **Single jump**

This is the jump you have in Dog's Dinner – you can only jump if you're on the ground. You go up and then down, but in some games you can steer left and right during the jump.

▽ **Double jump**

This is the jump you had before you fixed the infinite jumping bug – you can jump again in the air to go higher. In some games there are limits on double jumping – for example, you can only do it if you're going up.

▽ **Wall jump**

When you touch a wall, you can jump up again. Ninja-type characters often have this power. It's not very realistic but it's lots of fun!

Falling off the level

Platform games are all about staying on the platforms. Add the next script to the PlayerBlock to make the game end if it falls to the bottom of the stage.

25 Make a new block called "Fallen off", shown below, to check whether the PlayerBlock is at the bottom of the stage. Add it to the "forever" loop. Then build the short script at the bottom of the page to stop the sprite when it gets the "GameOver" message. Test the new code: the controls should stop working when you hit the deck.

Drop this block inside the "forever" block.

This block broadcasts the message when the sprite is less than 20 steps from the bottom of the stage.

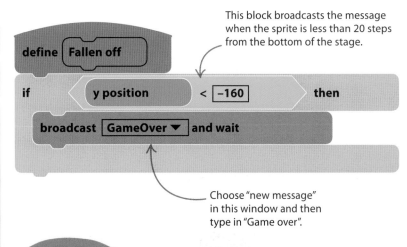

Choose "new message" in this window and then type in "Game over".

The "stop" block prevents the player from moving any further.

Adding a character

A red square isn't a very interesting main character for a platform game. You need something fun that you can animate. It's time to introduce the dog.

Time for me to disappear!

This block makes the dog face to the right at the start.

Costumes for walking animation

Delete this costume.

New costume:

1
dog2-a
127x110

2
dog2-b
127x104

3
dog2-c
121x109

duplicate

delete

save to local file

26 Click the sprite symbol in the sprites list to add a new sprite from the library. Select Dog2 and click "OK". Dog2 is a great sprite to use as it has more than one costume, which means you can animate it.

27 You only need Dog2's first two costumes for now, so go to the Costumes tab and delete the last costume (dog2-c).

when [flag] clicked

set rotation style [left-right ▼]

set size to (50) %

point in direction (90 ▼)

show

forever

The "go to" block places the dog on the red square.

go to [PlayerBlock ▼]

go to front

The dog appears in front of the red square.

if < key [left arrow ▼] pressed? > then

point in direction (-90 ▼)

next costume

The dog faces left if the left arrow key is pressed.

if < key [right arrow ▼] pressed? > then

point in direction (90 ▼)

next costume

The "next costume" blocks animate the dog's walk.

28 Add the script on the left to Dog2. It sticks the dog to the front of the red PlayerBlock so that it moves with it on the stage. The dog switches continually between its two costumes when you press the left and right arrow keys, which makes it look like it's walking.

Look – I'm walking!

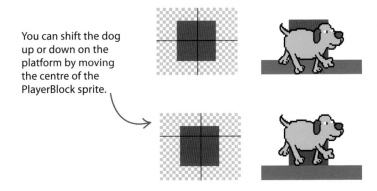

You can shift the dog up or down on the platform by moving the centre of the PlayerBlock sprite.

29 Run the project – the dog will now run around the stage with the PlayerBlock. If its paws are too low down on the platform, you can raise the centre point of the PlayerBlock costume (since the dog sticks itself to the PlayerBlock). The dog is just decoration, so it doesn't really matter if its paws stick out as it walks. It's the red square that's doing all the collision detection.

Collision detection

Collision detection – knowing when and how two objects are touching – is a big programming challenge when building games. This book mostly uses simple collision detection, but Dog's Dinner uses a collision-detection sprite.

▽ Simple collision detection

This method simply checks whether the player sprite is touching a hazard. It's fine for simple games, but without extra code you don't know which part of the player is touching and how much is overlapping. And animating the sprite may mean its paws stick out when you swap costumes, creating false collisions.

▽ Collision-detection sprite

Using a simple rectangle with an animated sprite on top (like our red square and blue dog) avoids the problem with costumes, because the PlayerBlock is always the same shape and size. But you still don't know which part of it has been touched. Programming tricks like our reversing script can solve some of the problems.

▽ Bumper sprites

You can surround the player with "bumper" sprites that move with it and detect collisions in each direction. Knowing which direction you've hit something allows you to bounce off it correctly. Extra sprites and scripts are needed for this type of detection.

▽ Mathematical collision detection

If you know where everything in the game is and exactly what size it is, then by using clever maths you can work out when and how things hit each other. But be warned: this can get really complicated, as you can see below!

if sqrt((dogx–jellyx)^2+(dogy–jellyy)^2) < (dogR+jellyR) then BUMP!

Howling dog

To give your blue dog more personality, make him howl with disappointment when the game ends.

Scripts | Costumes | Sounds

New costume:

dog2-c

1

Howling Dog
121x109

30 Load the Dog2 sprite from the library again as a new sprite, but keep only the dog2-c costume this time. Rename the sprite "Howling Dog". Load the "wolf howl" sound from the sound library.

Delete the dog2-a and dog2-b costumes, because you only need dog2-c.

The Howling Dog sprite is hidden until the message "GameOver" is broadcast.

31 Add these two scripts to make Howling Dog appear when the game ends.

```
when     clicked
hide
set size to (50) %
set rotation style [ all around ▼ ]
```

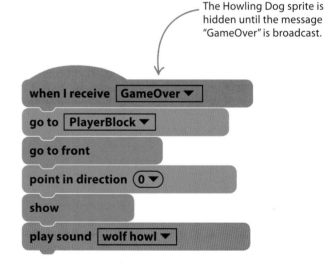

```
when I receive [ GameOver ▼ ]
go to [ PlayerBlock ▼ ]
go to front
point in direction ( 0 ▼ )
show
play sound [ wolf howl ▼ ]
```

32 Add the short script below to the original Dog2 sprite (not the new Howling Dog sprite) to make it vanish when Howling Dog appears. Run the project and see what happens when the dog falls off the platform.

```
when I receive [ GameOver ▼ ]
hide
```

Here we go again!

Making the levels

The next step is to create the game's three levels. You'll need to draw the platforms for each level by hand, matching the pictures on the next three pages as closely as you can. (You'll add the sprites later.) Skip forward to page 148 to find out how to paint the platforms – you can refer back to pages 145–7 once you've started.

▽ **Level 1**
Simple coloured steps allow the dog to hop downhill, collecting bones. Watch out for the donut, which slides left and right – you need to choose just the right moment to drop past it.

To help show where the platforms go, this image includes Scratch's xy-grid. To see the grid when you draw the platforms, select the stage info area in the lower left and click on the backdrop symbol to open the backdrop library. Scroll to the end and choose "xy-grid". It isn't essential to do this, but you might find it handy. You can replace the xy-grid with colour backgrounds after you've made the platforms.

▽ Level 2

On Level 2, the platforms are arranged like the rungs of a ladder. You need to position the platforms very carefully so the dog can drop down without getting stuck but without making it too easy.

▽ **Level 3**

On the last level, some players will be tempted to try to jump over the donut, but it's a trap! It's much easier to collect the first bone and then go back left to avoid the donut altogether.

Drawing the platforms

Now to create the platforms. Dog's Dinner has three levels, so you need to create three sets of platforms. Each one will be a costume in the Platforms sprite.

Create a new message called "Setup", which we'll use later to reset the game each time it starts.

This block changes the coloured backgrounds.

33 Create a variable called "Level" for the game's three levels. Uncheck the tick box so it doesn't show on the stage. To make the game use the correct level costume, add this script to the Platforms sprite. Before you start drawing, click once on this script with the mouse. This runs just this script, centring the sprite on the stage so that platforms will appear in the correct position when you draw them.

```
when I receive  Setup ▼

switch backdrop to        Level

go to x: (0) y: (0)

switch costume to         Level
```

This block changes the platforms.

34 With the Platforms sprite selected, click on the Costumes tab and then use the paintbrush symbol to create three new costumes. Delete the old test platform costume. Then use the rectangle tool to draw the platforms on each level. Try to match the pictures on the previous pages. Don't worry about getting them perfect, as you can adjust them later.

Name each costume.

Use the rectangle tool.

Don't add colour to the checked area.

The "Select" tool lets you select and move a platform.

Select solid colour.

Make sure you're in "Bitmap Mode".

35 To add colour to the backgrounds, select the stage info area to the left of the sprites list and then the Backdrops tab. Use the fill tool to fill the paint area with colour. Then click on the "Paint new backdrop" symbol to make a new backdrop and fill it with a different colour. Repeat to make a third backdrop.

Click here to paint a new backdrop.

Make sure the costumes appear in the correct order here. You can drag and drop them to change the order.

Creating a game control sprite

To make the levels change and set the start positions of all the objects on each level, you will need to build a control script. It's a good idea to keep this script in its own sprite.

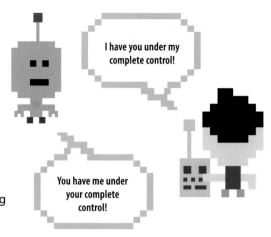

I have you under my complete control!

You have me under your complete control!

36 Create two variables, "Bones" (to count the number of bones left on the level) and "LevelOver" (to show when the player has finished the current level). Uncheck their tick boxes. Make an empty sprite using the paintbrush symbol in the sprites list. Name it "Game Control". Add the following script. It's a loop that repeats for every level. You also need to make two new messages: "Start" and "Win".

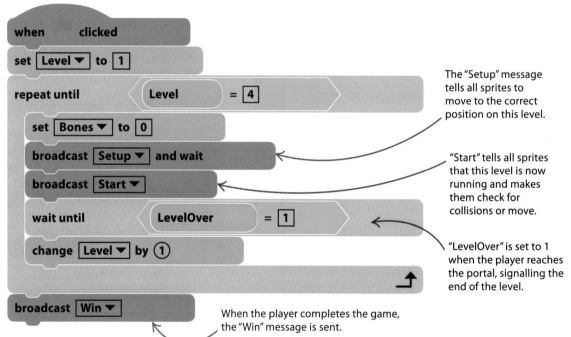

The "Setup" message tells all sprites to move to the correct position on this level.

"Start" tells all sprites that this level is now running and makes them check for collisions or move.

"LevelOver" is set to 1 when the player reaches the portal, signalling the end of the level.

When the player completes the game, the "Win" message is sent.

△ **How it works**

This script goes once round the loop for each level of the game. Then it moves on to the next block, which broadcasts a "Win" message to say that the player has won. The first broadcast is the message "Setup", which gets the sprites and background in position ready for the start of this level. It waits for all the receiving blocks to finish setting up before moving on. Then the "Start" message is sent. This triggers all the working scripts for the level, which move the sprites and look out for collisions.

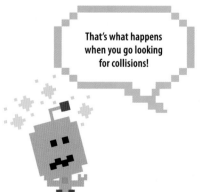

That's what happens when you go looking for collisions!

37 Change the PlayerBlock's main script so that the Game Control sprite's loop can trigger it with the "Start" message.

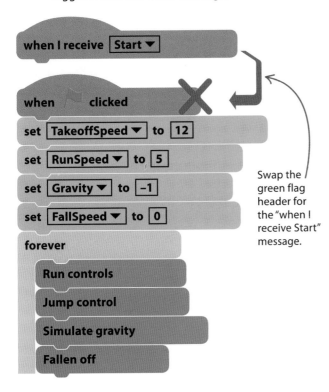

Swap the green flag header for the "when I receive Start" message.

38 With the PlayerBlock sprite still selected, add this next script to set its start position for each level when the "Setup" message is received. The script starts by ghosting the sprite completely, so that you only see the dog, not the red square. Ghosting is different from hiding a sprite because collisions can still occur – which is exactly what we want!

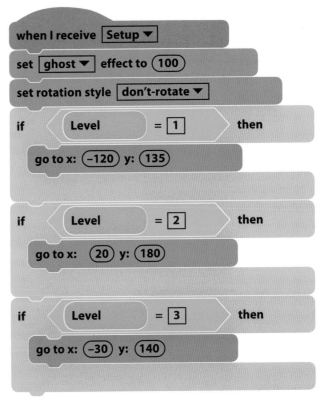

39 You also need to change Dog2's script so that it's triggered by the "Start" message.

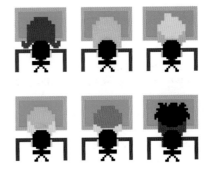

Placing the portals

Your game needs portals for the player to be able to progress through the levels. A portal is like a doorway that opens up when the player has completed a level.

40 Try running the project again. You should be able to run and jump on the Level 1 platforms, but at the moment there's no way to get to Level 2. Click the sprite symbol 👤 in the sprites list to open the sprite library. Add Button1 to your game and change its name to "Portal".

41 The portal needs a "Setup" script to position it correctly in each level and to make it slightly see-through before it opens.

"LevelOver" is set to 0 to show that the level is not over because the bones haven't been collected.

The "ghost" block makes the portal slightly transparent.

The "set color effect to" block is set to 0, which means that the sprite appears in its normal green colour at the start of each level.

The "go to" blocks set the portal's position on the stage for each level. Don't worry if the portal isn't in quite the right place – we'll fine-tune everything later.

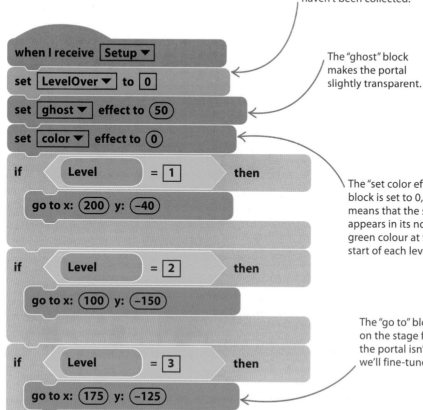

```
when I receive  Setup ▼

set  LevelOver ▼  to  0

set  ghost ▼  effect to  50

set  color ▼  effect to  0

if      Level      = 1    then
    go to x: 200  y: -40

if      Level      = 2    then
    go to x: 100  y: -150

if      Level      = 3    then
    go to x: 175  y: -125
```

42 The Portal's second script waits for the bones to be collected and opens the Portal by showing it changing colour until the player touches it. Run the game. We haven't added bones to the game yet, so the portal will open immediately. You should be able to run through all the levels. If you can't, go back and carefully check all the steps.

The open portal is no longer ghosted.

Setting "LevelOver" to 1 triggers a change of level.

The portal changes colour until the player touches it.

LINGO

Flags

"LevelOver" is a variable that the portal's script uses to tell the Game Control sprite when the level is complete. (Remember the "wait until" block in the Game Control sprite's loop? It makes the script wait before switching to the new level.) "LevelOver" allows different parts of a program to communicate. Programmers call a variable used in this way a "flag", and it is an alternative to using a message.

When "LevelOver" is 0 (because the level isn't over), we say that the flag is unset. When "LevelOver" is 1 (because the player has reached the open portal), we say that the flag is set. Messages can only start scripts, but by using a flag you can pause a script in the middle until something happens. In the Game Control sprite's loop, the "wait until" block pauses until the flag equals 1.

Flag unset
LevelOver = 0

Flag set
LevelOver = 1

Bones for the dog

It's not much fun just racing through the levels without having anything else to do. Let's add some bones that the dog must collect to open the portal. After all, he's getting hungry!

43 Create a new sprite and draw a bone about the same size as the dog. Use the paintbrush tool for the black outline and the fill tool to colour it white. Call it "Bone1". Don't forget to centre it.

Bone1

44 Add the script on the right to set Bone1's position on each level. The x and y coordinates determine where this bone will appear on the stage at each level of the game. The positions may not match your platform designs exactly, but they'll be fine for now.

BONE 1

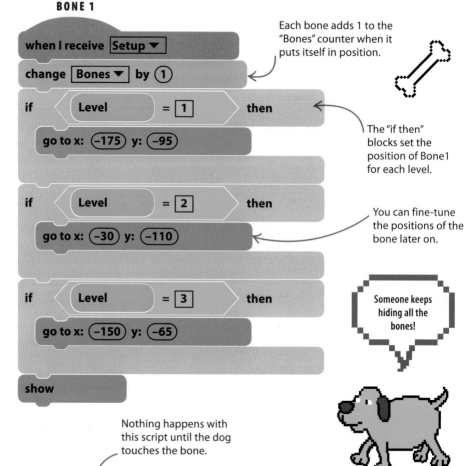

Each bone adds 1 to the "Bones" counter when it puts itself in position.

The "if then" blocks set the position of Bone1 for each level.

You can fine-tune the positions of the bone later on.

Someone keeps hiding all the bones!

Nothing happens with this script until the dog touches the bone.

```
when I receive Start ▼
wait until    touching PlayerBlock ▼ ?
hide
change Bones ▼ by -1
play sound dog1 ▼
```

The number of bones to collect falls by 1.

45 Add the "Start" script shown on the left to Bone1 to make it hide when the dog collects it. It also updates the "Bones" counter. Load the sound "dog1" to this sprite, so the dog gives a happy "woof" when he gets a bone. Run the project. At the moment, you should only have to collect one bone before the portal opens.

46 The game needs more than one bone, so right-click on the Bone1 sprite and select "duplicate". Do this twice. This will give you three bone sprites.

That's more like it!

47 You need to change the "Setup" scripts for Bone2 and Bone3 so that they appear in different places to Bone1 on each level. Change the numbers in the "go to" blocks to match those shown here.

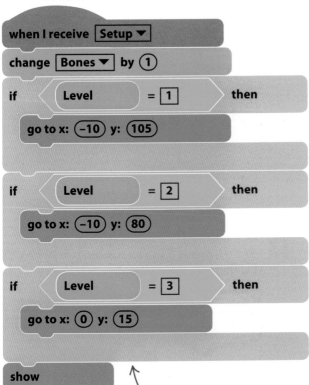

BONE 2

when I receive Setup ▼

change Bones ▼ by 1

if Level = 1 then
  go to x: (-10) y: (105)

if Level = 2 then
  go to x: (-10) y: (80)

if Level = 3 then
  go to x: (0) y: (15)

show

These blocks test which level the bone is on and set its position on the stage.

BONE 3

when I receive Setup ▼

change Bones ▼ by 1

if Level = 1 then
  go to x: (35) y: (-70)

if Level = 2 then
  go to x: (60) y: (-60)

if Level = 3 then
  go to x: (120) y: (140)

show

48 The bones' scripts manage the number of bones on a level automatically. Run the project. You should find that the portal won't open until you've collected all three bones.

Junk food

The dog is having a rather easy time of it with all those bones to eat. Adding some obstacles and hazards will make the game more difficult. Start with the flying donut.

49 Go to the sprite library, select Donut, and then click "OK" to load it into the game.

Load this donut sprite.

Donut

50 Now add this "Setup" script to shrink and position the donut for each level.

This sets the donut at the correct size.

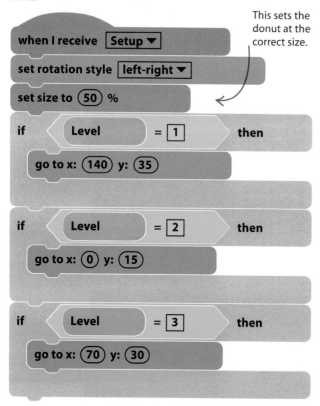

```
when I receive Setup ▼
set rotation style left-right ▼
set size to (50) %
if < Level = [1] > then
    go to x: (140) y: (35)
if < Level = [2] > then
    go to x: (0) y: (15)
if < Level = [3] > then
    go to x: (70) y: (30)
```

51 Next, add this "Start" script to get the donut patrolling back and forth.

```
when I receive Start ▼
forever
    point in direction (90 ▼)
    repeat (35)
        move (3) steps
    point in direction (-90 ▼)
    repeat (35)
        move (3) steps
```

Patrol to right

Patrol to left

52 Add one last script to detect a collision with the PlayerBlock and end the game – junk food really is bad for you!

```
when I receive Start ▼
wait until < touching PlayerBlock ▼ ? >
broadcast GameOver ▼
```

53 Now run the game and try getting past the donut. If you hit the donut, the dog will stop and howl.

ARRRRGH! JUNK FOOD!

Hazardous snacks

As well as the flying donuts there are a number of fixed traps on the levels. To keep things simple, all these hazards are part of a single sprite with three different costumes – one for each level.

This script ends the game if the dog touches a hazard.

54 Create a new blank sprite called "Hazards" and add the two scripts shown here. The "Setup" script selects the correct costume for the level and centres it on the stage (just like in Platforms). Click on the "Setup" script to centre the sprite before you design its costumes.

55 You need three costumes for the Hazards sprite. Use the paintbrush symbol to create two extra blank costumes. Select "costume1" and click the "Add" button at the top. Load the "cheesy-puffs" costume from the library. Use the "Select" tool to make it smaller and position it as shown here. Then, from the costume library, add two cakes to "costume2" and one to "costume3". Make them smaller and position them. You can fine-tune their positions later.

Most of the costume should have the checked pattern for a see-through colour.

Use a bowl of cheesy-puffs in Level 1.

Use two cakes in Level 2.

Use one cake in Level 3.

Fine-tuning

Now that your platforms, portals, bones, and hazards are all in roughly the right place, run the project and see if the game works. You might find that some sprites aren't positioned correctly. The game might be too tricky or the dog might get stuck. If so, you need to fine-tune your levels. The hints and tips here will also be handy if you want to design new levels.

Click and drag the small squares to stretch and resize the selection.

56 Most problems can be fixed by adjusting the positions and sizes of the platforms. Select the Platforms sprite and click the Costumes tab. Use the "Select" tool in the paint editor to move, stretch, or resize the Level 1 platforms. Click outside the selection box to show your changes on the stage. Adjust the platforms until Level 1 matches page 145.

To move a platform, click inside the selection and drag.

57 Use the same method to fine-tune the position of the Hazards sprite. Select it in the sprites list and click on the Costumes tab. Use the "Select" tool to adjust the position of the snack in the first costume (which appears in Level 1). Click outside the selection box to check your changes on the stage.

Fine-tune the cheesy-puffs using the "Select" tool.

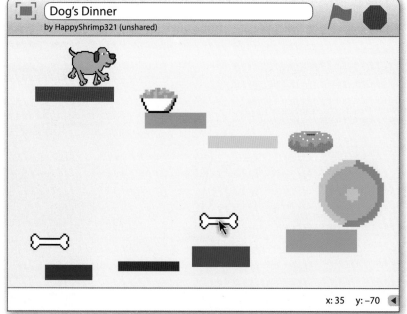

Dog's Dinner
by HappyShrimp321 (unshared)

x: 35   y: −70

58 You can reposition all the other sprites by using their x and y coordinates. Select a sprite on the stage and drag it where you want. Hover the mouse-pointer over the centre of the sprite and make a note of the x and y numbers that appear under the stage. Copy the numbers into the blue "go to" block in the sprite's Level 1 script.

if   Level   = 2

go to x: 35 y: −70

Copied numbers go here

The "go to" trick

To reposition a sprite perfectly, use this cunning trick. First drag the sprite on the stage to where you want it. Then look at the unused "go to" block in the Motion section under the Scripts tab. The sprite's coordinates will have appeared automatically in this block. Now you can simply drag the block into your script without needing to do any typing. Easy!

Drag sprite to new position

The bone's new coordinates appear automatically in the "go to" block in the blocks palette.

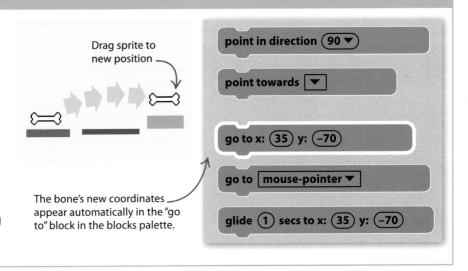

59 If you need to move the sliding donut, bear in mind that the "go to" block sets its start position. To change how far it slides, adjust the numbers in its two "repeat" loops. One controls how far it goes to the right, the other to the left.

60 You should now have Level 1 working beautifully. To work on another level and its sprites, you can make a temporary change to the script for the Game Control sprite. Change the number in the "set Level to" block to "2". Run the game and Level 2 appears on the stage. Fine-tune your sprites' positions. But remember to change the number in "set Level to" back to "1" when you're done.

Change the "1" to the level you want to work on, and that's where the game will start.

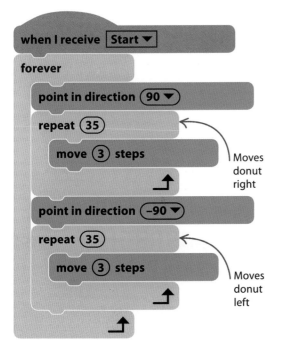

Moves donut right

Moves donut left

Signs and music

The game won't be complete until you've added some instructions and other messages for the player. You can also load some music into it to make it even more entertaining.

61 To give instructions and other messages to the player, use the paintbrush symbol to create a new blank sprite and call it "Signs". Add the costumes below to the Signs sprite. Name them "Instructions", "Win", and "Lose".

62 To show the correct sign to the player when the Signs sprite receives a message, add the three scripts below. Run the project to check that the correct signs show as you play.

The instructions vanish when the player's sprite touches them.

Instructions

DOG'S DINNER   MOVE: ARROW KEYS
                      JUMP: SPACE KEY

COLLECT ALL BONES   DOG DOES NOT LIKE
TO OPEN PORTAL TO   JUNK FOOD!
NEXT LEVEL

Win

YOU WIN!

Lose

ARRRRGH!
JUNK FOOD!

63 Check the positions of the instructions. You may need to rearrange them so that they don't overlap the images on the stage.

Altogether now!

Dog's Dinner
by HappyShrimp321 (unshared)

DOG'S DINNER

MOVE: ARROW KEYS
JUMP: SPACE KEY

COLLECT ALL BONES
TO OPEN PORTAL TO
NEXT LEVEL

DOG DOES NOT LIKE
JUNK FOOD!

64 You can give each level its own music. Select the Game Control sprite and load these sounds from the Scratch sound library: "xylo2", "xylo3", and "xylo4". The script below will swap the music each time you change level.

The first "repeat" loop plays "xylo2" until the player reaches Level 2.

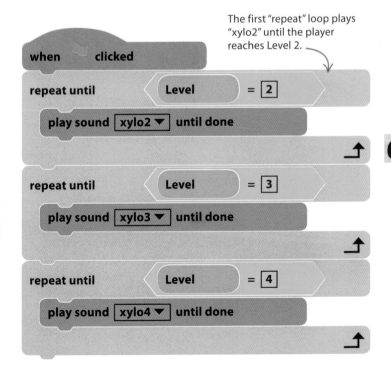

```
when [flag] clicked
repeat until < Level = 2 >
    play sound [xylo2 ▼] until done
repeat until < Level = 3 >
    play sound [xylo3 ▼] until done
repeat until < Level = 4 >
    play sound [xylo4 ▼] until done
```

65 Add the next script to the Game Control sprite to swap the music at the moment the new level starts and to announce the start of each level with a sound effect. Load the "space ripple" sound into the sprite.

```
when I receive [Start ▼]
stop all sounds
play sound [space ripple ▼]
```

66 To play a victory tune when the dog finishes the final level, load "triumph" from the sound library and add this script to the Game Control sprite. Run the game. Check that the music changes for each level, and that sound effects play at the start of each level and at the end of the game.

```
when I receive [Win ▼]
stop all sounds
play sound [triumph ▼]
```

Hacks and tweaks

Congratulations, your platform game is up and running! Test it and ask your friends to play it. You may need to adjust the sprites' positions and edit your platforms and hazards a little to make the game play smoothly and to get the difficulty level just right.

EXPERT TIPS

Backing up

Save a backup copy of the game under a different name before you start making changes. If you do this, you'll always have the copy to go back to if you make mistakes when tweaking the code. To save with the online Scratch editor, select the File menu and click on "Save as a copy".

▽ **Victory dance**

If you think the end of the game isn't exciting enough, change the script for the "Win" message to do something more spectacular. Maybe the dog could do a little victory dance? Why not add a new sign for when the dog falls off the platforms and ends up at the bottom of the stage? You could make the dog disappear too.

◁ **Extra levels**

To make the game longer you could create extra levels. You would have to give the Platforms and Hazards sprites more costumes, and edit the scripts to add "if Level =" blocks to place the bones, portal, and donut at the start of each level. Don't forget to change the "Level = 4" block in the Game Control sprite's loop, so that the game will end after the player has completed all the new levels.

▷ Mega-challenge

Can you figure out how to give the dog a limited number of lives? You'd need a new variable called "Lives", and you'd have to reprogram all the "GameOver" messages to subtract 1 from the variable until you reach the last life. The Game Control sprite's loop would also need changing. It's an expert programming challenge that needs clear thinking and hard work!

Increasing this number makes the dog jump higher.

```
when     clicked
set  TakeoffSpeed ▼  to  12
set  RunSpeed ▼  to  5
set  Gravity ▼  to  -1
```

Decreasing this number makes the jumps less floaty.

◁ Adjust the jump

You have total control over the dog's jumps. You can make him leap higher by increasing the value of the "TakeoffSpeed" variable. You can also make the value of "Gravity" smaller or larger to control how floaty each jump is. Why not add a special level with reverse gravity, so that gravity pulls you up, not down? You will need to make code changes to set the jump variables just for that level with an "if then" block, and also to detect when the dog "falls" off the top of the level!

▪▪▪ GAME DESIGN

Designing levels

Designing how all the challenges and rewards in a level fit together is a tricky job. You need to plan every detail and get a friend to test it to see if it's too easy or too hard. Make sure you can complete the level yourself before asking them to try it.

Timing Are your moving hazards going so fast you can't get past them, or so slow there's no challenge? Adjust their speeds until you're happy with them.

Are your hazards moving too fast?

Spacing Is the player able to jump from platform to platform easily – or perhaps too easily? Make the gaps between the platforms bigger or smaller to suit the level you're designing.

Tricks Try fooling the player into following what appears to be an obvious way through a level but then turns out to be a trap. The correct way will be an easier but less obvious, solution.

I've unlocked my tools!

Tools Computer games often come with level design tools that are unlocked once you finish the game. Using these you can create your own challenges and puzzles within the game. You can usually share your customized levels online, so that others can try them.

Glacier Race

How to build Glacier Race

Glacier Race is a two-player game in which you race up the screen, swerving round obstacles and collecting gems as you go. There's no finish line in this race – the winner is simply the person with the most gems when the time runs out.

Name of the game.

The player with the most gems wins the game.

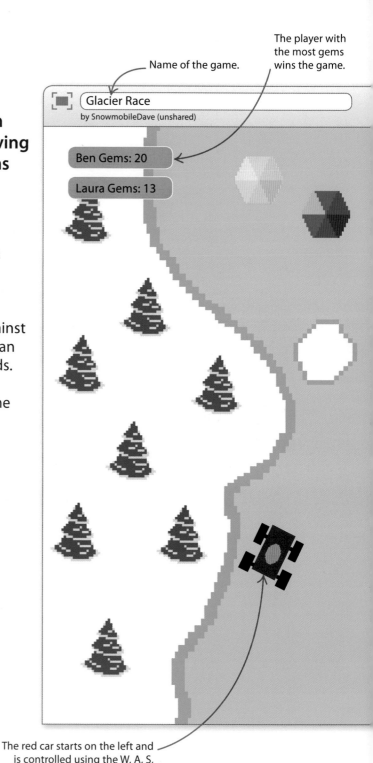

Glacier Race
by SnowmobileDave (unshared)

Ben Gems: 20

Laura Gems: 13

The red car starts on the left and is controlled using the W, A, S, and D keys on the keyboard.

AIM OF THE GAME

It's red car versus blue car in a race-off against the clock. Win by collecting more gems than your opponent before the countdown ends. Every gem you grab adds an extra second to the race countdown, but stay clear of the snow or you'll end up in a spin.

◁ **Cars**
Use the game controls to keep your car on the ice and collect gems. You can also push the other car off the road to gain an advantage.

◁ **Obstacles**
Avoid the giant snowballs and the edge of the road or you'll spin out of control.

◁ **Penguin**
The penguin is the master of ceremonies. He asks the players' names at the start, gives instructions, and announces the winner at the end.

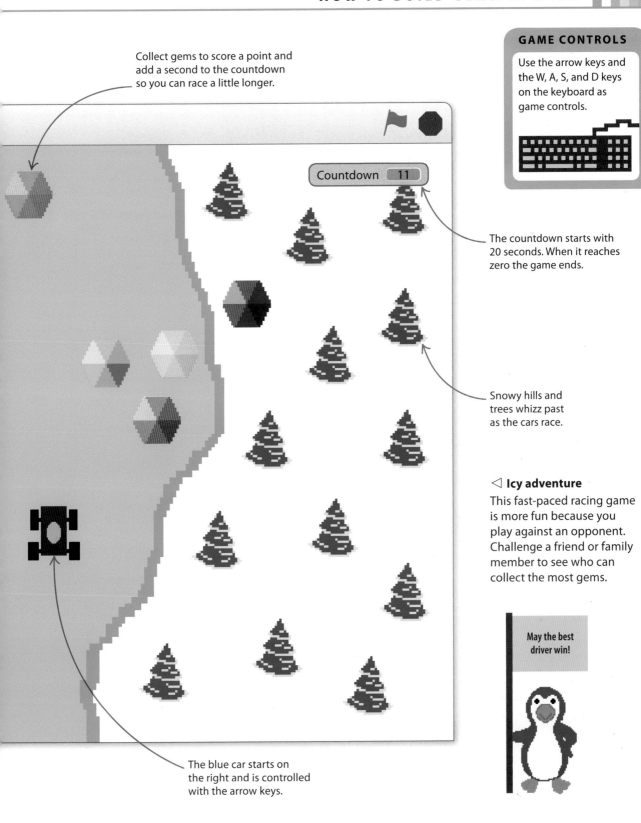

Collect gems to score a point and add a second to the countdown so you can race a little longer.

GAME CONTROLS

Use the arrow keys and the W, A, S, and D keys on the keyboard as game controls.

Countdown 11

The countdown starts with 20 seconds. When it reaches zero the game ends.

Snowy hills and trees whizz past as the cars race.

◁ **Icy adventure**
This fast-paced racing game is more fun because you play against an opponent. Challenge a friend or family member to see who can collect the most gems.

May the best driver win!

The blue car starts on the right and is controlled with the arrow keys.

The game loop

Fast games need clever code. This game uses something called a "game loop" to keep all the action happening just when it should. It's as if the game loop bangs a drum, and with each beat all the other sprites move one step. Start by creating a blank sprite to hold the game loop's script.

 Start a new project and delete the cat sprite. Use the paintbrush symbol / to create a blank sprite and rename it "Game Loop". Then make a variable for all sprites called "Countdown" for the game timer and show it on the stage. Build the following script to make the game loop. You'll need to create the messages "Setup", "Calculate", "Move", and "GameOver".

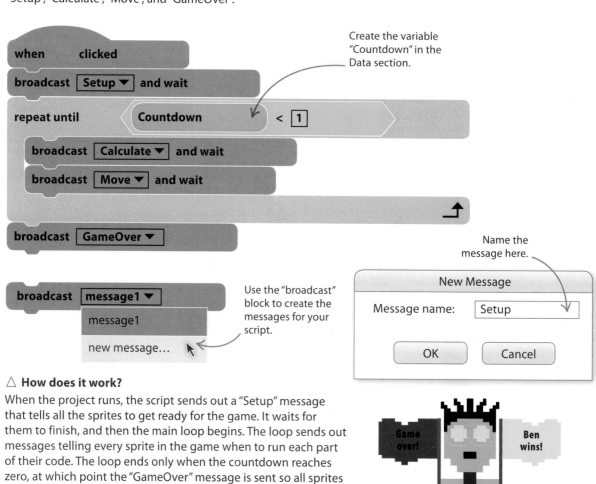

Create the variable "Countdown" in the Data section.

Name the message here.

Use the "broadcast" block to create the messages for your script.

New Message

Message name: Setup

OK   Cancel

△ **How does it work?**

When the project runs, the script sends out a "Setup" message that tells all the sprites to get ready for the game. It waits for them to finish, and then the main loop begins. The loop sends out messages telling every sprite in the game when to run each part of their code. The loop ends only when the countdown reaches zero, at which point the "GameOver" message is sent so all sprites can perform any final actions and the winner is announced.

Game loops

Using one main loop to keep everything in sync is common in computer games. The loop keeps all the sprites in step and makes the code tidy and short. It also helps the game run quickly – in Glacier Race, the game loop runs as fast as 30 times per second. In Scratch, a program with lots of sprites each with their own loops can become slow as the computer has to constantly jump between them. Using a single game loop fixes this problem, but be careful not to use loops elsewhere in the game as they will slow it down.

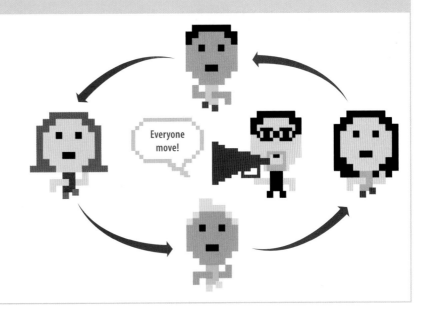

Everyone move!

2 Create two new variables for all sprites: "RoadY" (to store the y coordinate used to position our moving scenery) and "CarSpeed" (to set how quickly the cars can move around the stage). Uncheck the tick boxes in the Data section so they aren't displayed on the stage. Add the script on the right to set the values of the variables at the start of the game.

```
when I receive  Setup ▼
set  RoadY ▼  to  0
set  CarSpeed ▼  to  5
set  Countdown ▼  to  20
reset timer
```

This block sets the time limit for the game in seconds.

3 Add another variable for all sprites called "RoadSpeed" to store the speed of the moving scenery. Uncheck the tick box. Then create a script to calculate the position of the road each time the game loop runs. You'll see how this works once you've made the road sprites.

The y coordinate of the road decreases from 360 to −360 before jumping back to 360 as the road repeats itself.

```
when I receive  Calculate ▼
set  RoadSpeed ▼  to  -5
change  RoadY ▼  by      RoadSpeed
if      RoadY          < -360     then
    change  RoadY ▼  by (720)
```

Scrolling road

In Glacier Race, players feel as if they're moving quickly along the road, but in reality their cars don't move very far on the stage – it's the road that moves instead. The road is made up of two sprites that fit together seamlessly: Road1 and Road2. These roads take turns scrolling down the stage, making the cars appear to move faster than they really are.

Road2

The highlighted area is visible on the stage.

Road1

The cars appear to move forward as Road1 and Road2 move down the stage.

The two road sprites join perfectly with each other.

4 Create a new sprite and call it "Road1". In the paint editor, choose the paintbrush tool ✎ and set the thickness slider to the middle. Draw the edges of the road and make sure they run right from the top to the bottom without any gaps. Then use the fill tool ◆ to colour the area on both sides of the road white, creating a snowy setting.

costume1

Clear   Add   Import

Flip up-down

Fill these areas in with white.

Leave the road empty.

Thickness slider

Bitmap Mode

Convert to vector

100%

5 Now duplicate the Road1 sprite to make Road2. Select Road2 and go to the Costumes tab. Click on the "Flip up-down" button at the top right and the road costume will turn upside down. The edges of Road1 and Road2 will now match as they are mirror images. They'll look odd on the stage at the moment, but you'll fix that later.

Sprites

Road1   Road2

Use this tool to flip the costume upside down.

6 Add these scripts to Road1 to get the road moving. They position the road using the "RoadY" variable in the game loop. Try running the project – half the road will scroll down the screen.

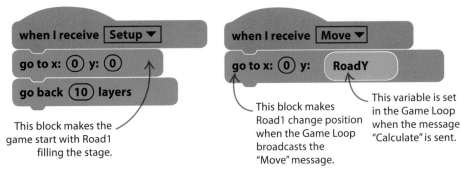

when I receive | Setup ▼ |

go to x: ⓪ y: ⓪

go back ⑩ layers

This block makes the game start with Road1 filling the stage.

when I receive | Move ▼ |

go to x: ⓪ y: ⟨ RoadY ⟩

This block makes Road1 change position when the Game Loop broadcasts the "Move" message.

This variable is set in the Game Loop when the message "Calculate" is sent.

7 Now build the following scripts for Road2 to make the second road sprite work together with the first. Run the project – the road should scroll smoothly down the screen.

when I receive | Setup ▼ |

go to x: ⓪ y: ③⑥⓪

go back ⑩ layers

This makes sure the scenery stays behind the other sprites.

Road2 is positioned above or below Road1, depending on where Road1 is on the stage.

when I receive | Move ▼ |

if ⟨ RoadY ⟩ < ⬛0 then

go to x: ⓪ y: ⟨ RoadY ⟩ + ③⑥⓪

else

go to x: ⓪ y: ⟨ RoadY ⟩ – ③⑥⓪

8 To add colour to the road, paint the backdrop rather than the sprites, or else the cars will collide with the road surface. Select the stage and click on the Backdrops tab. Use the fill tool ◈ to fill it with an icy blue colour.

backdrop 1
480x360

. . . LINGO

Scrolling

Moving everything on the screen together in the same direction is called scrolling. In Glacier Race, the road scrolls downwards. You might have heard of games called side-scrollers, which means the scene moves left or right as the player moves the character on the screen.

9 Make the scenery more interesting by adding some trees. Select Road1 and click on the Costumes tab. Click the "Add" button on top and add the tree costume. Shrink it by using the selection box and place it on the snow. Add as many trees as you like. Repeat the process for Road2.

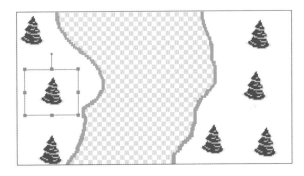

Race cars

It's now time to add the race cars. Once you've got one car moving, you can duplicate it to make the second one and save yourself a lot of work.

10 Click the sprite symbol 🐱 and load Cat1 from the library – you can use this sprite to ensure the car is the right size. Now open the paint editor and click on "Convert to bitmap". Use the rectangle and circle tools to draw a car like the one shown here. Make sure you draw the car facing right or it will point the wrong way in the game. Remember to delete the cat image once you've finished and use the "Set costume centre" tool to centre the car.

Use the rectangle tool to draw the body and wheels of the car.

Make your race car a bit bigger than the cat. The next script will shrink it.

Use the circle tool to draw an oval shape.

11 Rename the sprite "RedCar" in the sprites list. Then create a new variable, "spinning", which you'll use later to say when a car is in a spin. Note that for this variable, you need to select the option "for this sprite only" and uncheck the tick box in the Data section so that the variable doesn't show on the stage.

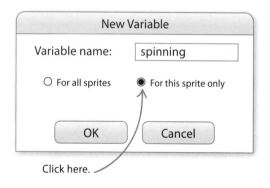

New Variable

Variable name: | spinning

○ For all sprites   ● For this sprite only

OK   Cancel

Click here.

12 Remember that in this project, sprites can run scripts only when they get messages from the Game Loop. Add the following script to set up the red car at the start of the game.

```
when I receive  Setup ▼
set size to (30) %
show
go to front
go to x: (-40) y: (0)
point in direction (0 ▼)
set  spinning ▼  to (0)
```

The script runs when the "Setup" message is sent by the Game Loop at the start of the game.

The car doesn't spin when the "spinning" variable is set at zero.

13 You now need to add keyboard controls for the car. Choose More Blocks in the blocks palette and then click on "Make a Block". Create a new block called "car controls" and add this script to its "define" block.

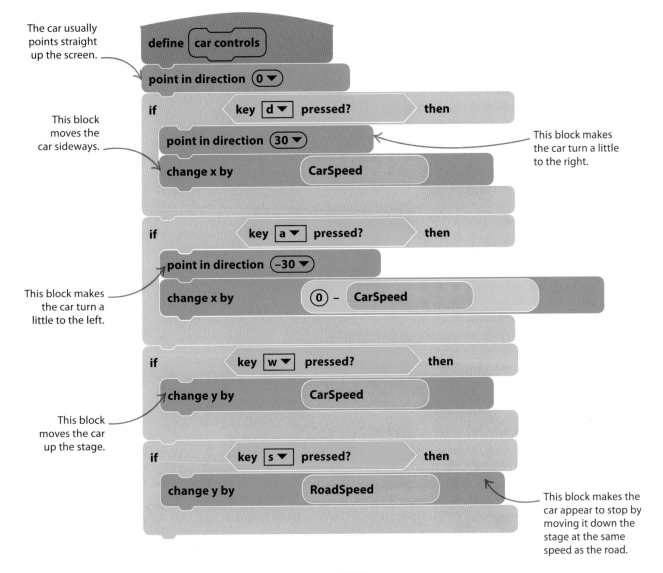

The car usually points straight up the screen.

This block moves the car sideways.

This block makes the car turn a little to the right.

This block makes the car turn a little to the left.

This block moves the car up the stage.

This block makes the car appear to stop by moving it down the stage at the same speed as the road.

14 Add a script to run the "car controls" block when the car receives the message "Move" from the Game Loop. Run the project. You should now be able to steer the red car along the road using the keys W, A, S, and D.

The "Move" message is sent by the Game Loop many times per second.

Collisions and spins

To make the game challenging, you can force players to avoid the snow by making their cars spin out of control if they touch it. You need to create some more new blocks to make this work.

Road hog!

15 With RedCar selected, create a new block to detect the snow. Choose More Blocks in the blocks palette and then click "Make a Block". Name the block "check collisions" and create the following script.

The "touching" block only detects the painted parts of the road sprite's costume, not the road itself.

```
define check collisions

if   touching Road1 ?   or   touching Road2 ?   then
        set spinning to 30
```

This block tells the car how long to spin for.

16 Now create another block, call it "spin", and add the script shown here. The "spin" block runs when the car is spinning. It turns the car round and reduces the "spinning" variable by one. When the variable reaches zero, the spin ends and the car is reset at the bottom of the stage.

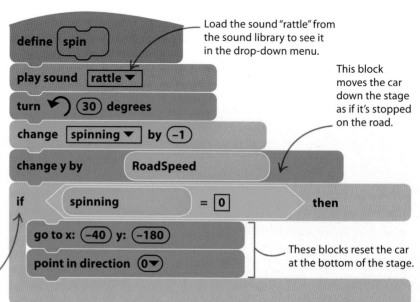

Load the sound "rattle" from the sound library to see it in the drop-down menu.

This block moves the car down the stage as if it's stopped on the road.

```
define spin

play sound rattle

turn ↺ 30 degrees

change spinning by -1

change y by RoadSpeed

if   spinning = 0   then
        go to x: -40 y: -180
        point in direction 0
```

These blocks reset the car at the bottom of the stage.

This block checks if the spin is over.

17 Finally, change the existing script triggered by the "Move" message to look like the one shown here. Now you can only control the car if the "spinning" variable is zero. Collisions are checked only when you're not in a spin – otherwise you'd spin forever! Run the game. The car should spin if it hits the snow.

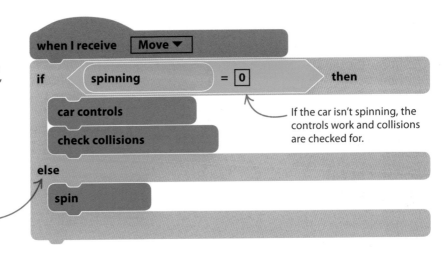

If the car isn't spinning, the controls work and collisions are checked for.

If the value for "spinning" is more than zero, the car will spin.

```
when I receive  Move ▼

if      spinning      = 0      then

    car controls

    check collisions

else

    spin
```

18 To add some snowball obstacles, create a new sprite in the paint editor. Make it about the size of the car on the stage. To get the correct size, watch it appear on the stage after you've drawn it. You can also see the costume's size in the costume list – aim for about 40x40. Name the new sprite "Snowball".

New costume:

costume1   Clear   Add   Import

1

costume1
40x40

These numbers show the costume's size.

19 Add the following three scripts to the Snowball sprite. The Snowball sprite is cloned to make lots of obstacles, but you might notice that there's no "create clone" block here. The clones will be created by the Game Loop sprite, using some code that we'll add next.

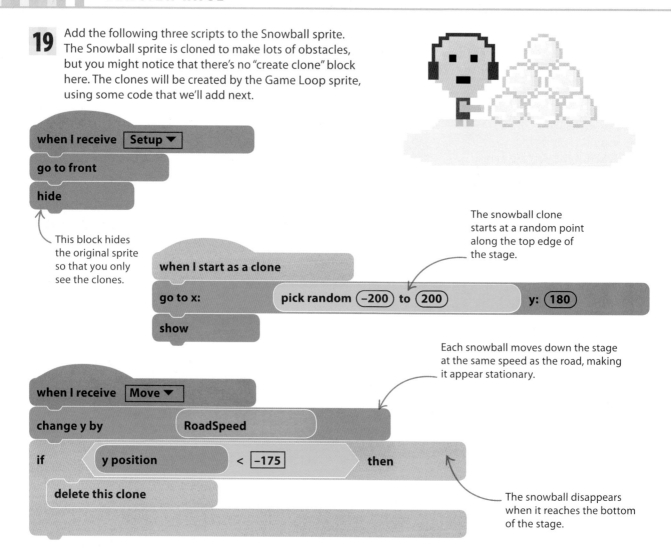

when I receive [Setup ▼]

go to front

hide

This block hides the original sprite so that you only see the clones.

when I start as a clone

go to x: (pick random (-200) to (200)) y: (180)

show

The snowball clone starts at a random point along the top edge of the stage.

when I receive [Move ▼]

change y by (RoadSpeed)

if ((y position) < [-175]) then

　delete this clone

Each snowball moves down the stage at the same speed as the road, making it appear stationary.

The snowball disappears when it reaches the bottom of the stage.

20 Now select the Game Loop sprite and add this script to make a new snowball appear with a chance of one in 200 every time the loop repeats.

Making this number bigger creates fewer snowballs.

when I receive [Move ▼]

if (pick random (1) to (200) = [1]) then

　create clone of [Snowball ▼]

21 To make the car spin when it hits a snowball, you need to add the Snowball sprite to the list of possible collisions for the red car. Run the game. You should now see the car spin when it hits a snowball.

Slot one "or" block into another.

touching [Road1 ▼] ?   or   touching [Road2 ▼] ?

define (check collisions

if ⟨ ⟩ or ⟨ touching [Snowball ▼] ? ⟩ then

set [spinning ▼] to [30]

Player two

You now need to create the second player's car. Doing this is easy – you simply copy the first car, recolour it blue, and tweak the scripts.

22 Duplicate the RedCar sprite and name the copy "BlueCar". Note that the duplicate sprite gets its own copy of all the scripts. This includes a copy of the "spinning" variable (set to "for this sprite only"), which can be different from the red car's.

Sprites

RedCar

duplicate
delete
save to local file
hide

23 Select the BlueCar sprite and click on the Costumes tab to open the paint editor. Use the fill tool to change the car's colour.

Use the fill tool to paint the car blue.

24 Now select the Scripts tab to see BlueCar's
scripts. Change the x coordinates in its "go to"
blocks to 40 in both the "Define spin" script
and the "When I receive Setup" script. This
makes the blue and red cars start next
to each other.

Change the x
coordinate to 40.

```
go to front
go to x: ( 40 ) y: ( 0 )
point in direction ( 0 ▼ )
set  spinning ▼  to  0
```

Change the x coordinate
to 40 here too.

```
if <  spinning  = ( 0 )  > then
    go to x: ( 40 ) y: ( -180 )
    point in direction ( 0 ▼ )
```

Select the arrow keys in all
four "key pressed?" blocks.

25 In the "Define car controls"
script, change the "key
pressed" blocks so that
the blue car can be
steered using the arrow
keys on the keyboard.
Then run the game.
Both the cars should race
along the track, but they
can drive through each
other at the moment.

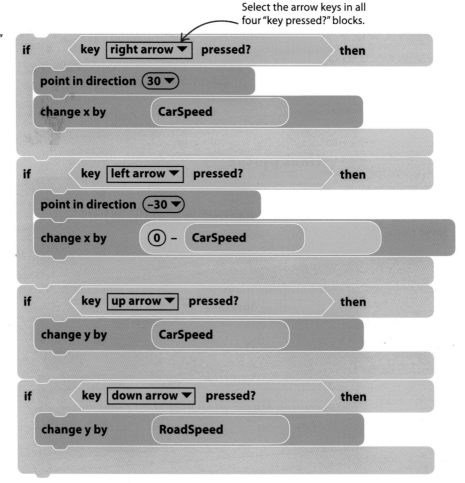

```
if < key  right arrow ▼  pressed? > then
    point in direction ( 30 ▼ )
    change x by  CarSpeed

if < key  left arrow ▼  pressed? > then
    point in direction ( -30 ▼ )
    change x by  ( 0 ) - CarSpeed

if < key  up arrow ▼  pressed? > then
    change y by  CarSpeed

if < key  down arrow ▼  pressed? > then
    change y by  RoadSpeed
```

▷ **Change the script**
In the "key pressed?" blocks,
replace key "d" with "right
arrow", key "a" with "left arrow",
key "w" with "up arrow", and
key "s" with "down arrow".

26 To stop the cars driving through each other, you need to make them sense each other and then bounce apart. Add a new "if then" block to RedCar's "Define check collisions" script as shown here. Create the message "bounce", and then add a new script to make RedCar move away from BlueCar when it receives the message.

Get out of my way!

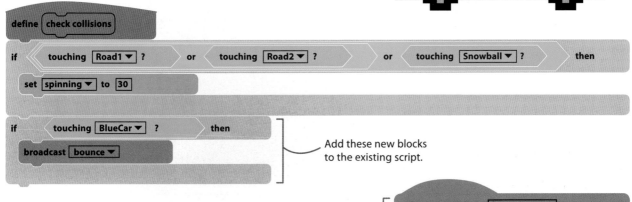

define check collisions

if ⟨ touching Road1 ▼ ? or touching Road2 ▼ ? or touching Snowball ▼ ? ⟩ then

set spinning ▼ to 30

if ⟨ touching BlueCar ▼ ? ⟩ then

broadcast bounce ▼

Add these new blocks to the existing script.

when I receive bounce ▼

point towards BlueCar ▼

turn ↻ 180 degrees

move 20 steps

point in direction 0 ▼

This new script makes RedCar bounce away from BlueCar.

27 Now make the same changes to BlueCar's scripts so it can sense when it touches RedCar and bounce. Run the game to check the cars bounce when they collide.

Choose RedCar here.

if ⟨ touching RedCar ▼ ? ⟩ then

broadcast bounce ▼

This time the "touching" block checks for collisions with the red car.

when I receive bounce ▼

point towards RedCar ▼

turn ↻ 180 degrees

move 20 steps

point in direction 0 ▼

Collecting gems

The next step is to create the colourful gems that the players battle to collect. Each gem will be a clone of a single gem sprite, which makes it easy to put lots of gems on the stage at once.

Use this tool to set the centre of the costume.

28 Click the paintbrush symbol in the sprites area to create a new sprite with the paint editor. To create a gem, use the line tool to draw six triangles arranged in a hexagon. Fill each one with a different shade of green. Make it similar in size to the snowball and centre it when you've finished.

costume1

Name the sprite "Gem".

Gem
40x33

29 Create two variables – "RedCarGems" and "BlueCarGems" (both for all sprites) – to tally how many gems each car collects. Now add these scripts to the Gem sprite; they're similar to the scripts for the snowballs.

```
when I receive Setup ▼
set RedCarGems ▼ to 0
set BlueCarGems ▼ to 0
go to front
hide
```

These blocks reset the scores when the game starts.

```
when I start as a clone
go to x: pick random -200 to 200    y: 180
set color ▼ effect to pick random -100 to 100
show
```

This block picks a random colour for the gem clones.

30 Add the following script to move the gems along with the road and to update the total number of gems collected by each car. Load the "fairydust" sound to the Gem sprite so that it plays each time a gem is collected.

This block moves the gem with the road so that it appears to be fixed in one spot.

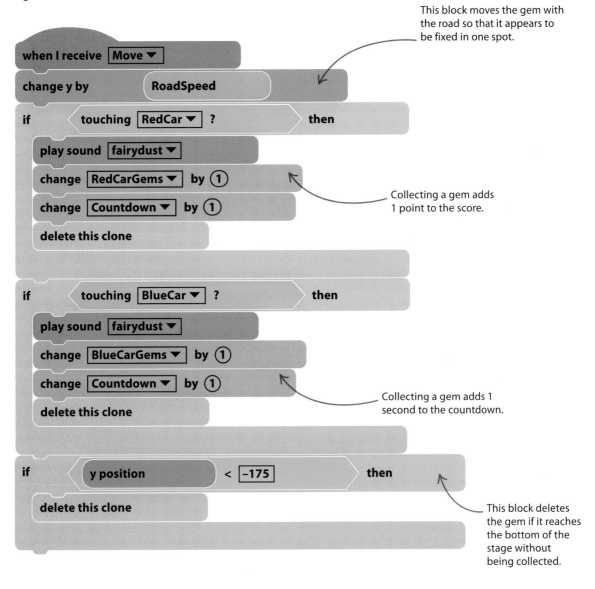

when I receive Move ▼

change y by (RoadSpeed)

if < touching RedCar ▼ ? > then

    play sound fairydust ▼

    change RedCarGems ▼ by (1)

    change Countdown ▼ by (1)

    delete this clone

Collecting a gem adds 1 point to the score.

if < touching BlueCar ▼ ? > then

    play sound fairydust ▼

    change BlueCarGems ▼ by (1)

    change Countdown ▼ by (1)

    delete this clone

Collecting a gem adds 1 second to the countdown.

if < (y position) < [−175] > then

    delete this clone

This block deletes the gem if it reaches the bottom of the stage without being collected.

31 In the Game Loop sprite, add a second "if then" block to the "when I receive Move" script to create the gem clones. Run the game and try collecting gems. The snowballs will stop players from rushing to the top and collecting all the gems. The gems and snowballs together create the balance and challenge of the game.

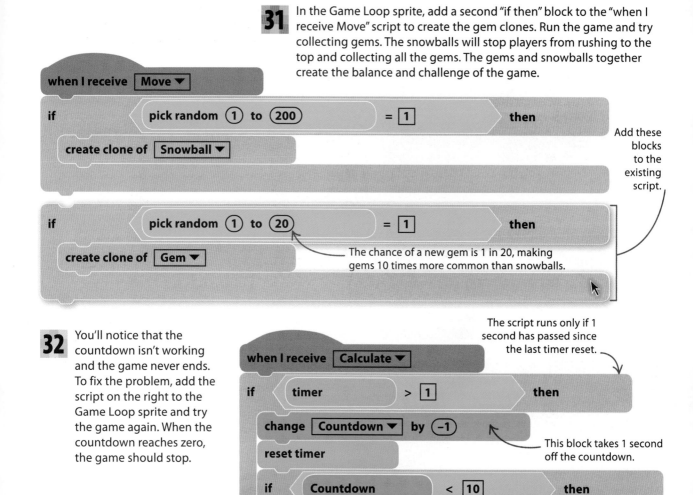

```
when I receive  Move ▼

if          pick random  1  to  200           =  1          then

    create clone of  Snowball ▼


if          pick random  1  to  20            =  1          then

    create clone of  Gem ▼
```

Add these blocks to the existing script.

The chance of a new gem is 1 in 20, making gems 10 times more common than snowballs.

32 You'll notice that the countdown isn't working and the game never ends. To fix the problem, add the script on the right to the Game Loop sprite and try the game again. When the countdown reaches zero, the game should stop.

The script runs only if 1 second has passed since the last timer reset.

```
when I receive  Calculate ▼

if        timer        >  1          then

    change  Countdown ▼  by  -1
    reset timer

    if        Countdown       <  10          then

        play sound  pop ▼
```

This block takes 1 second off the countdown.

This "if then" block plays "pop" sounds in the last 10 seconds of the game to warn the players time is running out.

Penguin in charge

A proper start and finish can make a game look more professional. Add a penguin race official to ask the players' names, start the race, and announce the winners.

33 First, create four variables for all sprites: "RedName" and "BlueName" to store each driver's name; and "RedInfo" and "BlueInfo" to show each driver's score during the race. Then add the Penguin2 sprite to talk to the players, and load the "gong" sound from the library to Penguin2.

Penguin2

34 Add this "Setup" script to the Penguin2 sprite. The Game Loop uses a "broadcast and wait" block, so the race doesn't start until the players put in their names and the penguin shouts "Go!"

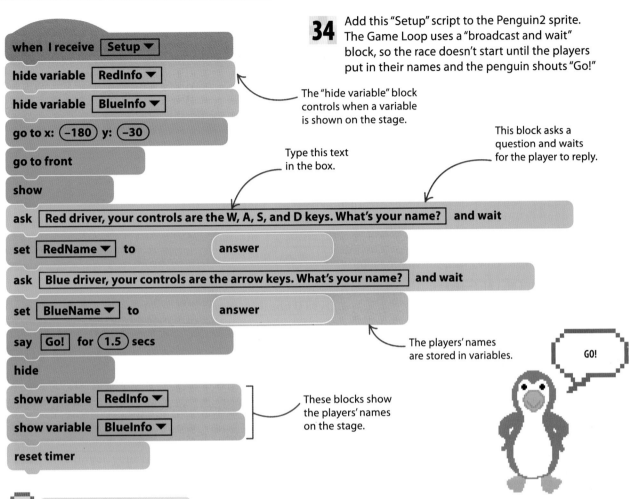

The "hide variable" block controls when a variable is shown on the stage.

```
when I receive  Setup ▼
hide variable  RedInfo ▼
hide variable  BlueInfo ▼
go to x: (-180) y: (-30)
go to front
show
ask  Red driver, your controls are the W, A, S, and D keys. What's your name?  and wait
set  RedName ▼  to  answer
ask  Blue driver, your controls are the arrow keys. What's your name?  and wait
set  BlueName ▼  to  answer
say  Go!  for (1.5) secs
hide
show variable  RedInfo ▼
show variable  BlueInfo ▼
reset timer
```

Type this text in the box.

This block asks a question and waits for the player to reply.

The players' names are stored in variables.

These blocks show the players' names on the stage.

GO!

EXPERT TIPS

The ask and answer blocks

A sprite can put a question to the person at the computer by using the "ask" block. Anything typed as the reply is stored in the "answer" block, which can then be used inside other blocks just like a variable can.

```
when       clicked
ask  How much is the cactus juice?  and wait
next costume
think  join  answer  ?? That's daylight robbery!
```

35 Add this script to the Penguin sprite to set the "RedInfo" and "BlueInfo" variables, which are displayed on the screen to show the scores.

> Type a space before "Gems:" so that it doesn't form a single word with the player's name on the stage.

```
when I receive  Calculate ▼

set  RedInfo ▼  to   join   RedName    join  Gems:   RedCarGems

set  BlueInfo ▼  to   join   BlueName    join  Gems:   BlueCarGems
```

36 Run the game. Hide all variables except "Countdown", "RedInfo", and "BlueInfo" by unchecking their tick boxes in the Data section. Then right-click the RedInfo and BlueInfo signs on the stage and choose "large readout". To make everything look tidy, drag the signs to the top left and move the countdown to the top right.

> Tick the check boxes to show the variable on the stage.

```
Make a Variable

☑  BlueInfo

☑  Countdown

☑  RedInfo
```

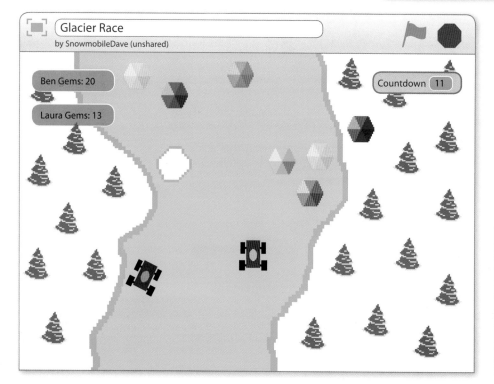

Glacier Race
by SnowmobileDave (unshared)

Ben Gems: 20

Laura Gems: 13

Countdown 11

. . . LINGO

String

Programmers call an item of data that contains words and letters a "string". It can include any character on the keyboard and can be of any length.

37 To make the penguin announce the winner, add the next script. This script has one "if then else" block inside another. Think about the three possible results – red wins, blue wins, and a draw – and it should all make perfect sense.

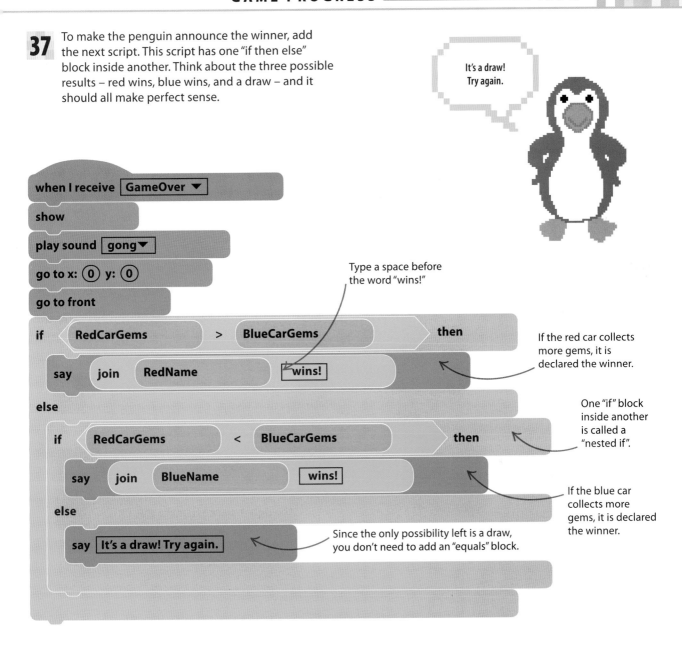

It's a draw!
Try again.

Type a space before the word "wins!"

If the red car collects more gems, it is declared the winner.

One "if" block inside another is called a "nested if".

If the blue car collects more gems, it is declared the winner.

Since the only possibility left is a draw, you don't need to add an "equals" block.

38 Finally, add some rhythmic dance music to make the game feel faster. Load "dance around" to the Game Loop sprite and then add this script. It's a loop, and extra loops can slow everything down, but since it only runs once every few seconds it won't affect the game play.

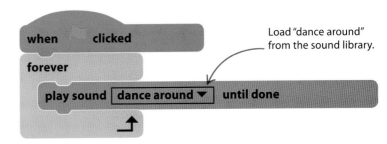

Load "dance around" from the sound library.

Hacks and tweaks

Now over to you! Personalize this race with your own features and adjustments. Make it as fast, slow, hard, fast, serious, or silly as you like.

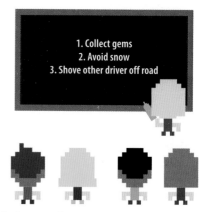

▽ **Record your own sounds**

You can use your own voice to make announcements in the game. To record your voice, you need a computer with a microphone. Select the Penguin sprite and click on the Sounds tab. Then click the microphone icon to make a recording. Replace the Penguin's "say" block with a "play sound" block and choose your recording.

Click here to make a recording.

△ **Instructions**

Remember to add instructions to the project page in Scratch. Make it clear that it's a competition to get the most gems and not a race to the finish line. Give players a helpful hint by telling them they can push the other player off the road.

▷ **Fine-tuning**

To change how hard or easy the game is, adjust the "CarSpeed", "RoadSpeed", and "Countdown" variables that are set at the start. You can also adjust how long the cars spin for after a crash, how big the bounce is when they collide, and how often snowballs and gems appear. Try to get just the right balance to make the game tricky, but not too hard.

△ **Change the scenery**

It's easy to change the setting of Glacier Race by repainting the scenery. You can make the players race through a desert canyon or a dirt track in a forest. Remember to change the snowballs to match your theme.

△ **One-player game**

Experiment with a one-player version of the game where you play against a computer-controlled blue car. First save a copy of the project so you don't spoil the two-player version. Change the car controls for the blue car, as shown here, and then try the game. The blue car will chase the red car and crash into it.

Insert these blocks into the second window of the "set RoadSpeed" block.

Put the "addition" block into the first window of the "division" block, and then insert it into the "subtraction" block.

△ **Need for speed**

For extra thrills, you can make the game speed up as players collect more gems. To do this, change the "set RoadSpeed" block in the Game Loop sprite so that the variable changes with each gem collected.

. . ▪ ▪ ▪ **GAME DESIGN**

Camera angles

Game designers often talk about the "camera" in a computer game. This refers to how the picture on the screen follows the action in the game. There is no real camera, but if you imagine a camera capturing the action, you can think about different ways of showing what's going on. Here are some common camera views in computer games.

◁ **Fixed**

The camera watches all the action from one spot, without moving. Most of the games in this book use this simple camera, either with a side or bird's eye view of the action.

△ **Tracking**

This camera follows the player around the game. In Glacier Race, the camera follows the cars, keeping them in view as the road moves past.

△ **First person**

This camera shows the view the player would see through their own eyes. First-person games make the player feel immersed in the action, rather than watching from afar.

△ **Third person**

This type of camera is positioned just behind the player's sprite. The player feels involved in the action, but can clearly see what the sprite is doing.

Tropical Tunes

How to build Tropical Tunes

Computer games aren't just about quick reflexes – they can also challenge your thinking powers. Here's a brain game to test how good your memory is.

AIM OF THE GAME

In Tropical Tunes, you have to listen to the drums play and then repeat the ever-growing tune. Make a mistake and the game's over. The longer you can match the tune for, the higher your score.

◁ **Listen**
The drums play a tune, starting with a single note and then adding one new note each time.

◁ **Drums**
Click the drums in order to repeat the tune the game plays to you.

◁ **Game over**
Make a mistake and the game ends. As the tune gets longer, the game gets harder.

Click this icon to make the game fill your screen.

You score a point each time you click on the correct drum.

Tropical Tunes
by CrazyDrummer123 (unshared)

Score   0

A tropical backdrop sets the scene, but the background in this game isn't important.

Click the green flag to start a new game.

GAME CONTROLS

Use a computer mouse or touchpad to play this game.

Click the stop sign to end the game.

The drums jump out when they play a note.

◁ **Harder and harder**

This game gets harder the longer you play. To help you remember the sequence, each drum plays a different note and has a different colour, but eventually you won't be able to remember the whole pattern!

How good is your memory?

Make a drum

This game is quite complicated, so you'll need to work through the instructions carefully. To get started, follow the directions to make one drum with all the scripts it needs. Once that's done you can copy it to make all four drums. Later, you'll create a game loop called the "master controller" to play the drums.

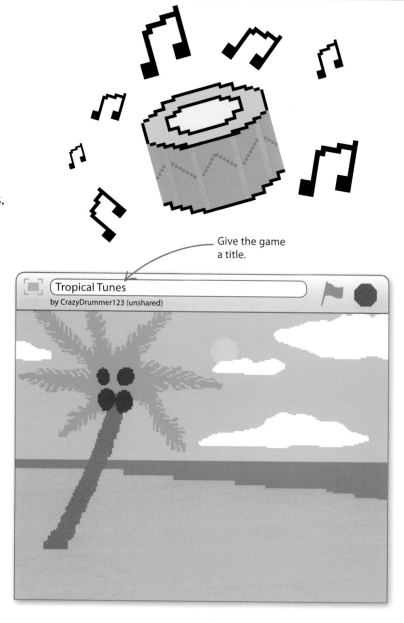

Give the game a title.

1   Create a new Scratch project and add or create any backdrop you want. A tropical theme works well with this game.

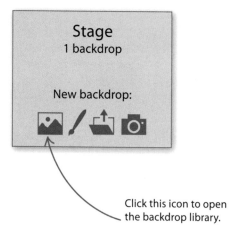

Stage
1 backdrop

New backdrop:

Click this icon to open the backdrop library.

2   The game needs four drums, but you can make just one to start with. Delete the cat sprite and add the "Drum1" sprite from the sprite library. Drag it to the lower left of the stage.

The name "Drum1" will be given to the sprite automatically.

Drum1

Two types of variable

You may have noticed the option to choose "For all sprites" or "For this sprite only" when you create a variable. So far you've mostly used "For all sprites", but you'll need to use both options in this game.

3 Before you can start making the scripts that bring the drum to life, you need to create some variables. Click on the Data section and make two variables for all sprites called "DrumToPlay" and "ClickedDrum". Uncheck their tick boxes. Every sprite in the game can use these variables.

Uncheck the boxes.

4 Now add three variables "For this sprite only". Call them "drumColour", "drumNote", and "drumNumber". These variables will store information about only Drum1: its number, its colour, and which note it plays. Using "For this sprite only" enables you to copy this sprite to make more drums later, while allowing each drum to have different values for these variables.

Uncheck the boxes here too.

5 Build the script below for Drum1. It sets up the drum's number, colour, the note it plays, and the type of sound it makes (like a steel drum). Run the project to set the variables and watch the drum change colour.

This drum's variable information is set up in these three blocks.

This selects the steel drum sound.

. . ▪ ▫ ▪ LINGO

Variables

Programmers have special terms for variables that apply to all sprites or only one sprite.

▷ Those that apply to only one sprite are called **local variables**.

▷ Those that apply to all sprites are called **global variables**.

To help you tell which is which, all the global variable names in this book start with a capital letter and local variable names don't.

Making your own block

In Dog's Dinner and Glacier Racer, you found out how to create your own customized Scratch blocks. You'll need to create a few more in this game.

6 Go to the blocks palette and select "More Blocks". The option "Make a Block" will be visible.

7 Select "Make a Block" and a box will pop up. Type in the name of your new block: "play drum". Then click "OK".

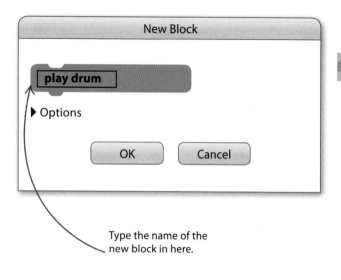

Type the name of the new block in here.

8 Next, the new block appears in the blocks palette and a special purple header block, "define play drum", appears in the scripts area.

9 Build this script below the "define play drum" block. Then, anywhere you use the "play drum" block, Scratch will run the script. The script will make the drum grow in size, play a note, and then shrink back to normal. You can test the new "play drum" block by clicking on it.

10 Now add this short script to Drum1. Click the drum on the stage to test it. Before testing, you'll need to click the green flag to set the value of drumNote.

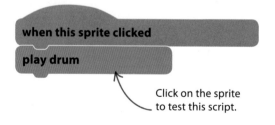

Click on the sprite to test this script.

Remote control drums

Tropical Tunes makes the drums play a sequence that the player has to copy. The game controls the drums by using a master controller to send messages to them and then wait for a reply. Before you set up the master controller, give Drum1 the scripts it needs to receive and broadcast messages.

11 Build this script, which will be triggered by a message called "RemoteControl". Create the message by selecting the drop-down menu on the "when I receive" block. Choose "new message" and type in "RemoteControl".

Create a new message called "RemoteControl".

```
when I receive  RemoteControl ▼

if  DrumToPlay  =  drumNumber  then

    play drum
```

▽ **How it works**

Eventually there will be four drums numbered 1 to 4 (the local variable drumNumber). Before the master controller broadcasts "RemoteControl" it will set the *global* variable "DrumToPlay" to the number of the drum it wants to sound, and only the matching drum will play. We will add these steps later.

This variable for all sprites tells the game which drum to play.

```
set  DrumToPlay ▼  to  2
broadcast  RemoteControl ▼  and wait
```

Don't add these blocks yet – we'll use them later.

MESSAGE

Only Drum2 plays, because its "drumNumber" matches "DrumToPlay".

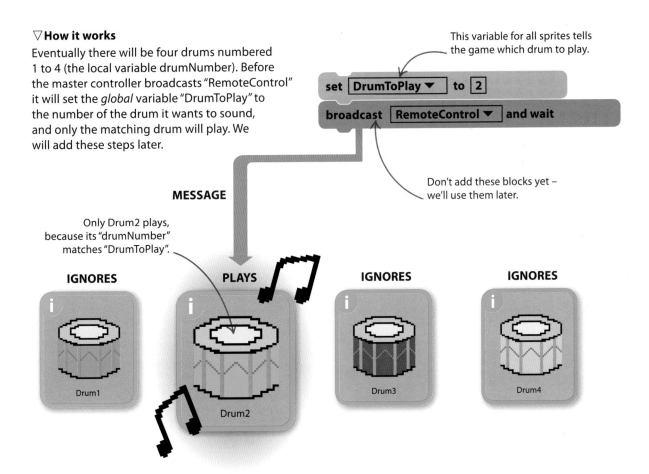

IGNORES — Drum1

PLAYS — Drum2

IGNORES — Drum3

IGNORES — Drum4

12 When the player clicks a drum, the master controller will need to check it's the right one. To make this work, you need to make the clicked drum do two things. First, it will change the global variable "ClickedDrum" to its own number. Then it will broadcast a message to make the master controller run its check. Change Drum1's "when this sprite clicked" script to look like this.

when this sprite clicked

set ClickedDrum ▼ to drumNumber

broadcast Clicked ▼

play drum

The drum changes the global variable "ClickedDrum" to its own number.

Create a new message and call it "Clicked".

Four drums

You now have one drum complete with its scripts. You can copy it three times to create the four drums you need for this game.

13 Duplicate the drum three times, then change the values of the three local variables as shown below to give each drum a different number, colour, and note. Arrange the drums on the stage, ordered from one to four.

Drum1

Drum2

Drum3

Drum4

when 🏳 clicked

set drumNumber ▼ to 1   to 2   to 3   to 4

set drumColour ▼ to 100   to 60   to 170   to 30

set drumNote ▼ to 60   to 62   to 64   to 65

14 Now run the project. Each drum should become a different colour. Click on them in turn to hear them play. If they move instead of playing, click on the blue full-screen symbol in the top left of the stage. Nothing else will work yet, but it's good to test that your drums all play correctly.

The master controller

Now you need to create the game's main brain: the master controller. The master controller broadcasts the "RemoteControl" message that plays the drums, but it does several other jobs too. It generates the drumbeat sequence the player has to follow; it checks the player has clicked the right drum; and it keeps track of the score. It will need several scripts to do all this.

15 The stage is a good place to put the master controller scripts as they don't belong to any one sprite. Click on the stage info area at the bottom left of the screen to choose the stage.

Click here to add scripts to the stage.

16 The master controller will keep track of the ever-growing sequence of drumbeats by storing them in a numbered list. To create the list, open the Data blocks section and click the "Make a List" button. Name it "DrumOrder" – it's going to store the order in which the drums will play. Check the tick box so you can see it on the stage.

Tick here to show the list on the stage.

17 With the stage selected, build this test script to generate a random sequence of seven drum numbers in the list. This script isn't part of the final game (for that, the script will need to add notes one by one). However, building it will show you how lists work and will let you try out the drums.

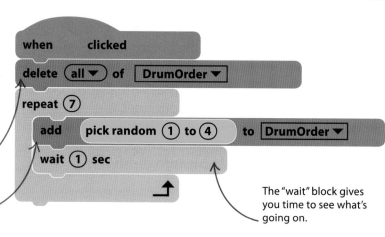

This block clears the list at the start of the test.

This block adds a random drum number to the end of the list.

The "wait" block gives you time to see what's going on.

18 Run the script and watch the "DrumOrder" list on the stage slowly fill up. It will look like this, but your numbers won't be the same. The drums don't play yet because there are no blocks to tell them to.

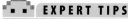

EXPERT TIPS

Lists

Making a list is a great way to store information, and lots of programming languages use them. They are handy for all sorts of things, from creating leaderboards and doing complex calculations to giving sprites artificial intelligence. In Tropical Tunes, we use a list to store numbers, but you can store words in lists too.

Lists are usually hidden, but you can display them on the stage just like variables.

You can use a list to make a sprite say something random when you click on it.

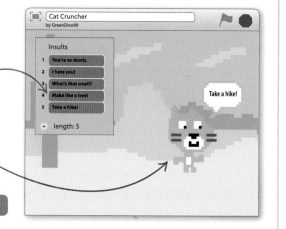

Commanding the drums

19 Now create another new block called "play sequence" and build the script shown here. It will play the notes in the list in order by travelling once though the blocks in the loop for each item in the "DrumOrder" list, setting "DrumToPlay" from the list, and then sending out the "RemoteControl" message. You will need to create a new variable for all sprites called "Count".

The "Count" variable keeps track as the program works down the list.

This block puts the drum's number in the "DrumtoPlay" variable.

This blocks tells the drums to play.

20 Add the new "play sequence" block to the test script.

Place the new "play sequence" block here.

▪▪▪ EXPERT TIPS

Broadcast blocks

There are two types of broadcast Scratch blocks. They are useful in different ways.

`broadcast Message ▼`

△ **Broadcast**
This sends the message but then continues straight to the next block without waiting. This is useful for triggering an event without stopping what's going on, such as launching an arrow without pausing the loop that moves the player's sprite.

`broadcast Message ▼ and wait`

△ **Broadcast and wait**
This sends the message but then waits until all receiving scripts have finished before running the next block. This is useful when you don't want the script to continue until something's finished, such as the drum playing in this game.

21 Now run the script. Watch the numbers alongside the items in "DrumOrder" light up as they are read by the script, then hear and see the correct drum play each time. You can check the "DrumToPlay" variable's tick box to show the number used with the "Remote Control" message for each note.

Select the tick box to show the "DrumToPlay" variable on screen.

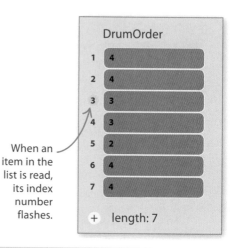

When an item in the list is read, its index number flashes.

Adding notes to the tune

So far you've just been testing the drums. It's now time to get them playing the sequences needed in the game, starting with one note and adding another note each time the player repeats the tune correctly.

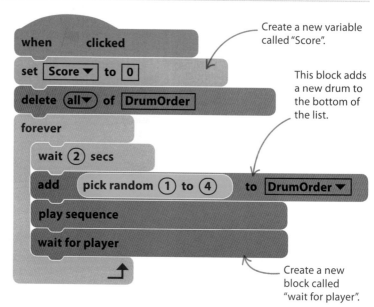

Create a new variable called "Score".

This block adds a new drum to the bottom of the list.

Create a new block called "wait for player".

22 The test script isn't needed any more so replace it with this one. You'll need to create another new block called "wait for player" – its script is shown in the next step. You'll also need to create a new variable for all sprites, called "Score", and check it so it appears on the stage.

23 Add a new variable called "CorrectCount" to count how many drums the player gets right. Then create this script, which holds up the loop while it waits for the player to get the whole drum sequence right.

24 If you run the project now, the drums will play one note and then wait. You can click as many drums as you like but nothing will happen because you haven't programmed the master controller to respond to the "Clicked" message yet.

Checking the player's tune

Now you need to add a script to respond to the player's clicks on the drums. Every click creates a "Clicked" message that can trigger a script to check which drum was clicked and count the number of correct clicks. If the player clicks the wrong drum, the script will broadcast a "GameOver" message.

25 Add the next script to the stage to increase "CorrectCount" by one for each correct click. When the drums are clicked, they play and send the "Clicked" message, having put their number in "ClickedDrum". This script will be triggered by that "Clicked" message. If the numbers don't match, the game ends.

This is the number of the correct drum held in the list.

This is the number of the drum you clicked.

Create a new message called "GameOver".

26 Add a game-over script to the stage. You'll need to load the "bell toll" sound to the stage from the Scratch sound library.

27 The game is complete. Now try playing it, but remember to uncheck "DrumOrder" in the Data section of the blocks palette or the player can just read the correct drum order off the list.

Uncheck the box to hide the drum order from the player.

▷ How it works

This game relies on two messages: "RemoteControl", which tells a drum to play, and "Clicked", which tells the master controller that a drum has been clicked by the player. The master controller has a loop that uses these two messages in turn – to play the tune and then check the player's reaction.

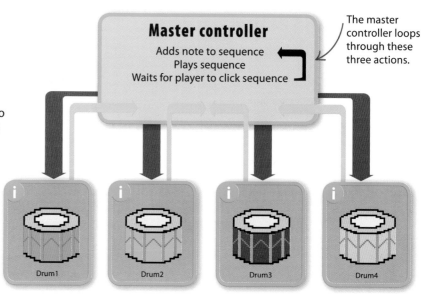

Master controller

Adds note to sequence
Plays sequence
Waits for player to click sequence

The master controller loops through these three actions.

 "RemoteControl" message makes the drums play.

 "Clicked" message tells the master controller when a drum is clicked.

Hacks and tweaks

Once everything is working smoothly, you can play around with the code and tweak the game to try and make it more exciting or harder. Here are some ideas.

Obey me!

△ Talking shark
Try adding a shark sprite that swims up and gives instructions – make him talk using the "say" block.

▽ Another drum
Add a fifth drum. You'll need to change its drum number, note, and colour values, and check anywhere in the code that thinks there are only four drums – such as the random block in the master controller.

14

△ Round counter
Create a new global variable "Round" and show it on the stage. Set it to zero at the start of a game and increase it by one every time the player completes a sequence correctly (at the end of the master controller loop).

GAME OVER!

◁ Game over
Add a game-over sign or make the shark swim back onto the stage to say it.

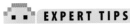 **EXPERT TIPS**

Debugging

Bugs are errors in programs. Getting rid of them is called debugging. If a program isn't working properly, there are a number of common Scratch problems you can check for, which are shown below. If you're following instructions and something isn't working, it's also worth going back to the beginning and checking all the steps – there could be a small mistake in one of your scripts that is affecting the whole game.

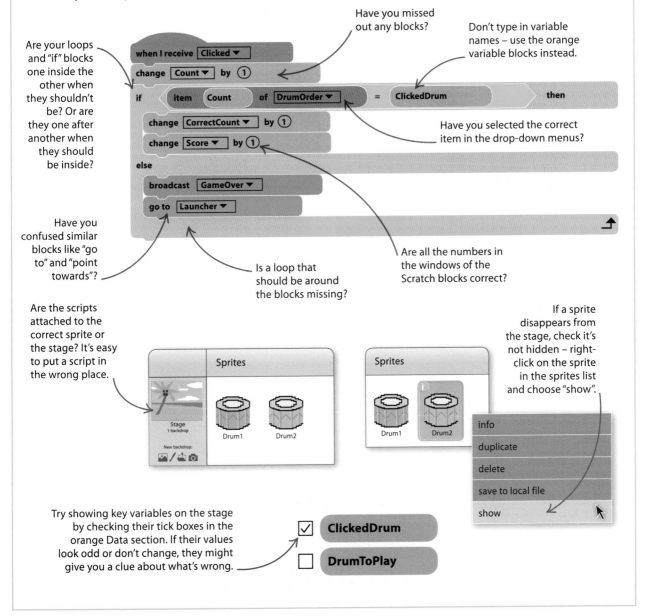

Are your loops and "if" blocks one inside the other when they shouldn't be? Or are they one after another when they should be inside?

Have you missed out any blocks?

Don't type in variable names – use the orange variable blocks instead.

Have you selected the correct item in the drop-down menus?

Have you confused similar blocks like "go to" and "point towards"?

Is a loop that should be around the blocks missing?

Are all the numbers in the windows of the Scratch blocks correct?

Are the scripts attached to the correct sprite or the stage? It's easy to put a script in the wrong place.

If a sprite disappears from the stage, check it's not hidden – right-click on the sprite in the sprites list and choose "show".

Try showing key variables on the stage by checking their tick boxes in the orange Data section. If their values look odd or don't change, they might give you a clue about what's wrong.

What next?

Remixing and beyond

The Scratch website allows you to see other users' code and reuse it in your own games; this is called remixing. Millions of projects have been shared online and you can dive into every one. It's a great place to share your games and find ideas.

Exploring Scratch

To see games shared by other Scratch users, go to the Scratch website at **www.scratch.mit.edu** and click on Explore.

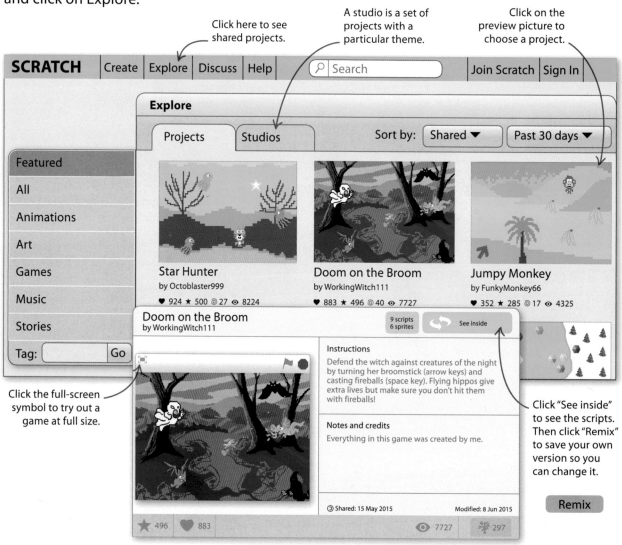

Click here to see shared projects.

A studio is a set of projects with a particular theme.

Click on the preview picture to choose a project.

Click the full-screen symbol to try out a game at full size.

Click "See inside" to see the scripts. Then click "Remix" to save your own version so you can change it.

SCRATCH   Create   Explore   Discuss   Help   Search   Join Scratch   Sign In

Explore

Projects   Studios   Sort by: Shared ▼   Past 30 days ▼

Featured
All
Animations
Art
Games
Music
Stories
Tag: Go

Star Hunter
by Octoblaster999
♥ 924 ★ 500 ◎ 27 👁 8224

Doom on the Broom
by WorkingWitch111
♥ 883 ★ 496 ◎ 40 👁 7727

Jumpy Monkey
by FunkyMonkey66
♥ 352 ★ 285 ◎ 17 👁 4325

Doom on the Broom
by WorkingWitch111

9 scripts
6 sprites   See inside

Instructions
Defend the witch against creatures of the night by turning her broomstick (arrow keys) and casting fireballs (space key). Flying hippos give extra lives but make sure you don't hit them with fireballs!

Notes and credits
Everything in this game was created by me.

Shared: 15 May 2015   Modified: 8 Jun 2015

★ 496   ♥ 883   👁 7727   ✳ 297

Remix

Creating your own games

Once you've built all the games in this book, you'll probably be bursting with your own game ideas. Here are some tips to help you get started.

1 **Big and small ideas**
Good ideas can come to you at surprising times, so be ready to jot them down before you forget them. Don't just keep notes about new games – write down ideas about smaller details such as characters, objects, levels, and actions.

2 **Beg, borrow, and steal**
People say the best ideas are stolen. Scratch allows you to steal ideas from everyone else, so go ahead. Look through other people's projects and save any sprites, costumes, backdrops, sounds, or scripts you like in your backpack, so you can reuse them later.

3 **Code your game**
Start with the basics. Begin by coding the main character so it works with your chosen controls (keyboard or mouse). Then build up slowly, adding one sprite at a time and creating the scripts it needs to play its part in the game.

4 **Testing**
Once you're happy with the game, ask someone else to play it. They might find problems that you missed because you know the game too well. Fix any bugs and make sure it all runs smoothly.

5 **Share it!**
Click the "See project page" button at the top right of the Scratch editor and add a few words to explain how to play the game. Then click on "Share" to allow the whole world to play your masterpiece. Well done, you are now a game maker!

See project page

Share

Better Scratch

Good programmers try to write code that's easy to understand and change. There are many ways in which you can improve your projects and expand your knowledge of Scratch. Here are a few of them.

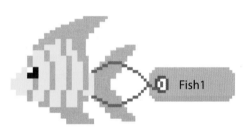

△ **Use clear names**
Scratch lets you choose names for sprites, variables, and messages. Make sure you use meaningful names, such as "Dragon" or "Score", to make your Scratch code readable.

△ **Comments**
You can add comments to any block to explain your code. To do this, just right-click on it and select "Add comment". This can help remind you when you read code written a while ago.

Setting a variable helps you change this number in just one place.

△ **No unexplained numbers**
Avoid writing code that contains unexplained numbers. To make your code easier to read, add a comment or use a variable so the number explains itself.

▽ **Backpack**
The backpack is a feature found at the bottom of the Scratch screen. It lets you store useful scripts, sprites, sounds, and costumes and move them from project to project. But remember that you can only use it online.

Drag and drop a script or sprite to copy it to the backpack.

Backpack

Sound
Scream-female

Costume
monkey2-a

Backdrop
Underwater2

Script

The help tool

Are you still unsure about how to use certain blocks? The help tool in Scratch will let you master the function of each block with ease.

1 To find out more about a particular block, first click the "Block help" symbol in the toolbar at the top of the screen.

"Block help" symbol

2 After the mouse-pointer turns into a question mark, click on any block in the blocks palette. A help window opens with tips on how to use that block.

The mouse-pointer turns into a question mark.

if on edge, bounce

If touching the edge of the stage, then bounce away

when [ ] clicked

forever

move (10) steps

if on edge, bounce

A help window opens.

The sprite will bounce at an angle if it is touching the **side**, **top**, or **bottom** of the stage

Making your project different

Scratch projects often look and sound similar if you only use resources from the Scratch library. To make yours different, import your own images and sounds into Scratch.

Click here to upload an image file from your computer.

Click here to use your webcam to take a picture.

Click here to use a sound file from your computer.

Use this to record sounds.

△ **Your own images**

You can import any image into Scratch, but don't share a project containing photos of people you know. You can also create your own images with a graphics program or the paint editor in Scratch.

△ **Your own sounds**

You can record your own music and sound effects through your computer's microphone and edit them in Scratch. You can also find free music and sounds on the web to use in your games.

The next level

Once you've made a few Scratch games of your own, you might want to expand your horizons. There's a whole world of knowledge and experience you can tap into to improve your game design and programming.

Game design

Begin by improving your knowledge of games and how they're created. The following activities will expand your imagination and stimulate your game-design brain.

◁ **Play games**

Playing games can trigger ideas for new ones. Try out different games and watch other people playing them. Think about the actions (mechanics), rules, and goals that make a good game work. Imagine how you might code these different parts of the game yourself.

△ **Learn from the experts**

Many game designers love to talk and write about how they design games. You can find their tips on video-sharing websites and in blogs and magazines.

▷ **Find stories**

Ideas for games and the characters in them often come from stories. Next time you watch a good film or read a good book, think how you might turn it into a game.

▷ **Explore gaming history**

Find out more about the history of gaming. Visit a video game museum or a vintage arcade. There are lots of free online versions of famous video games, so it's easy to try classic games this way.

GAME OVER!

△ **Think visually**

Thinking visually is a vital skill for a game designer. Practise drawing or try making models. To help create animations, film someone walking and then pause the video during playback to see their posture changing.

◁ **Keep notes**

Keep a notebook of game ideas, drawings, stories, and anything that you find fun or interesting – you never know what might be useful later. You could even start a blog about gaming to share your ideas with friends and family.

Programming

To make computer games, you need to know how to code. Brushing up your coding skills will allow you to make better games.

▷ Sharpen your Scratch

Try out the tutorials and explanations on the Scratch website. Learn everything you can about Scratch and you'll be able to code things you never dreamed possible.

△ Code together

Join or start a coding club at your school or library. Collaborating on projects with other coders is a great way to fire your imagination and supercharge your skills.

▷ Learn another language

Scratch is a great springboard to learn other programming languages, such as Python or JavaScript. There are lots of online coding courses, including some that focus on games. Python has a great add-on called Pygame that helps you create games.

△ Try a game engine

You don't have to build computer games from scratch – you can use programs called game engines to do a lot of the difficult coding for you. You can find game engines online. Many can be tried for free.

◁ Do your research

If you have a technical mind and want to learn more about the latest advances in computer games, read up on 3D graphics, game physics, and artificial intelligence.

 EXPERT TIPS

Game engines

A game engine is a program that contains ready-made code for building games. It works a bit like Scratch, but it's designed for professional game developers rather than beginners learning to code. Game engines provide easy ways to detect controller inputs and to guide sprites around the screen. Solutions to problems caused by collision detection and game physics are built in. Game engines can also convert games to run on consoles and mobiles, saving you the bother of rewriting all the code.

Jobs making games

Some computer games are created by a single programmer, but others are put together by huge teams. The computer games industry employs thousands of people. Most of them specialize in just one part of the process.

Who makes games?

Game studios are companies that make games and employ specialists to work as a team. On smaller games, each person usually has more than one job. On a big project, there might be dozens of programmers and artists, each working on just a small part of the game.

△ **Producer**

The person in charge of a project and all the people working on it is called a producer. It's their job to make sure the game is the best it can be.

△ **Writer**

The stories and characters in a game are developed by writers. In a game with cutscenes (short, movie-like sequences), the writer is responsible for what the characters say.

△ **Game designer**

The game designer creates the rules, goals, and mechanics that make a game interesting and fun for players. Playability is the designer's main focus.

◁ **Artist**

Everything the player sees – the characters, objects, and scenery – are created by artists, often working as a team under a single lead artist.

LINGO

Game types

Indie games Short for "independent games", these are created by people working on their own or by small teams. Many feature creative new ideas not seen in mainstream games.

AAA games These are the biggest games and are expected to sell millions of copies. They take many months or even years to make and have huge teams and budgets of many millions of dollars.

△ **Composer**

A composer is a professional musician who writes new music. Good music is vital as it helps create atmosphere in a game.

△ **Sound designer**

The sound effects in a game help to set the scene. They are created by a sound designer, who also decides how the composer's music will be used in the game.

△ **Programmer**

Programmers take all the ideas and building blocks created by the team and use them to write code that makes the game work.

△ **Tester**

It might sound like a dream job playing games all day, but it's a serious and important part of developing a game. A tester has to play the game over and over to check if it works correctly and is not too easy or hard.

△ **Game publisher**

Some games have a publisher – a company that pays for the game's development and then advertises and distributes the final product.

Game development

Games go through lots of different versions before the final one is released for sale. The early versions take the game from a basic idea to a finished product and usually follow the sequence shown here.

· · GAME DESIGN

From blocks to riches

In 2009, Swedish programmer Markus "Notch" Persson released the first version of Minecraft, a building game he'd made. By 2014, Minecraft had around 100 million registered users and was sold to Microsoft for $2.5 billion.

1 **Prototype**

The prototype is an experimental version of the game built to see if the basic idea works and is fun to play.

2 **Alpha**

The alpha version has all the main features, but they might not be fully working. They are improved and major bugs are fixed before the next stage.

3 **Beta**

The beta version of the game has everything, but it needs polishing and still has minor bugs, which need to be found and fixed.

4 **Release**

The release is the final version, fully tested and fixed. Some games are available as "early access" releases for fans to test before the game is 100 per cent finished.

Have fun!

Games can transport you to different worlds and take you through a whirlwind of emotions, but the most important part of gaming and making games is to have fun.

Party time!

Playing games with people is much more fun than playing on your own. Why not grab some snacks and invite your friends round to play your favourite multiplayer game? You could also get them to try out games you've made in Scratch and ask them to suggest improvements. They might even want to create their own versions.

Hold a game jam

A game jam is a game-making party. People get together for a day or two to race against time as they build a game from start to finish. Every year, countless game jams take place. Some take place in a single location, but others are scattered across the world and linked through the internet or even held entirely online. Why not hold a mini Scratch jam at your home or school? Pick a theme and ask a teacher or parent to help arrange computer access, judging, and prizes.

▷ **Choose a theme**
Game jams usually have a theme, such as "jumping games" or "games with bees in them". Prizes are awarded for building the best games.

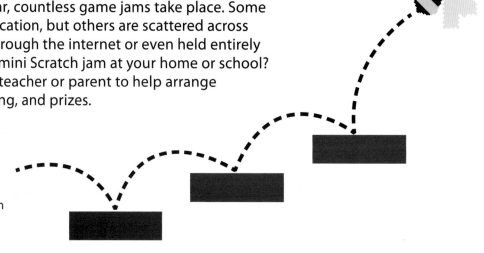

Challenge yourself

It's good to push yourself sometimes, so why not set yourself a game challenge? It could be anything from making a fully playable game in just 15 minutes to making a game for every letter of the alphabet. You could also keep a diary or blog to describe your experiences, or create a Scratch studio to share your challenge games.

Find or start a game club

If your school or library has a coding club, you can ask them to run some sessions on game design and programming. Start a group within the club for people who have a special interest in making games.

 EXPERT TIPS

Game idea generator

For some people, the hardest part of creating games is having the idea for a game in the first place. Here's a trick to help give you inspiration. Roll a dice to choose a number from each column, and then combine the results to generate a random game idea. Feel free to change it – it's just to get your creative brain in gear!

Genre

1. Maze
2. Jumping
3. Quiz
4. Vehicle simulator
5. Virtual pet
6. Interactive story

Setting

1. Forest
2. Space
3. Underwater
4. City
5. Castle
6. Beach

Extra feature

1. Patrolling enemies
2. High score
3. Collecting objects
4. Life counter
5. Time limit
6. Multiplayer

Glossary
and Index

Glossary

algorithm
A set of step-by-step instructions that perform a task. Computer programs are based on algorithms.

animation
Changing pictures quickly to create the illusion of movement.

artificial intelligence (AI)
Programming to make characters such as enemies in a game appear to behave in intelligent ways.

assets
All the pictures and sounds used in a game.

backdrop
The picture behind the sprites on the stage in Scratch.

backpack
A storage area in Scratch that allows you to copy things between projects.

block
An instruction in Scratch that can be joined to other blocks to build a script.

Boolean expression
A statement that is either true or false, leading to two possible outcomes. Boolean blocks in Scratch are hexagonal rather than rounded.

branch
A point in a program where two different options are available, such as the "if then else" block in Scratch.

bug
A coding error that makes a program behave in an unexpected way. Bugs are named after the insects that got into the wiring of early computers, causing errors.

camera
The imaginary camera through which a player views a game.

collision detection
Programming that detects when two objects in a game are touching.

condition
A "true or false" statement used to make a decision in a program. See also *Boolean expression*.

console
A computer that is used just for playing games.

costume
The picture a sprite shows on the stage. Rapidly changing a sprite's costumes can create an animation.

data
Information, such as text, symbols, or numbers.

debug
To look for and correct errors in a program.

directory
A place to store files to keep them organized.

event
Something a computer program can react to, such as a key being pressed or the mouse being clicked.

execute
See *run*.

export
To send something to the computer from Scratch, such as a sprite or a whole project saved as a computer file.

file
A collection of data stored with a name.

flag
A variable that is used to pass information from one sprite or script to another.

function
Code that carries out a specific task, working like a program within a program. Also called a procedure, subprogram, or subroutine.

game engine
A program that helps a programmer to make games by providing ready-made code for many common game features, such as animation, controls, and game physics.

game jam
A competition in which game makers race against the clock to build the best game.

game loop
A loop that controls everything that happens in a computer game.

game physics
Programming to create forces and collisions between objects in a game.

genre
A type of computer game. Platform games and first-person shooters are common genres.

global variable
A variable that can be changed and used by any sprite in a project.

graphics
Visual elements on a screen that are not text, such as pictures, icons, and symbols.

GUI
The GUI, or graphical user interface, is the name for the buttons and windows that make up the part of the program you can see and interact with.

hardware
The physical parts of a computer that you can see or touch, such as wires, the keyboard, and the screen.

header block
A Scratch block that starts a script, such as the "when green flag clicked" block. Also known as a hat block.

import
To bring something in from outside Scratch, such as a picture or sound clip from the computer's files.

index number
A number given to an item in a list.

input
Data that is entered into a computer. Keyboards, mice, and microphones can be used to input data.

integer
A whole number. An integer does not contain a decimal point and is not written as a fraction.

interface
The means by which the user interacts with software or hardware. See *GUI*.

library
A collection of sprites, costumes, or sounds that can be used in Scratch programs.

list
A collection of items stored in a numbered order.

local variable
A variable that can be changed by only one sprite. Each copy or clone of a sprite has its own separate version of the variable.

loop
A part of a program that repeats itself, removing the need to type out the same piece of code multiple times.

mechanics
The actions a player can do in a game, such as jump, collect objects, or become invisible.

memory
A computer chip inside a computer that stores data.

message
A way to send information between sprites.

network
A group of interconnected computers that exchange data. The internet is a giant network.

operating system (OS)
The program that controls everything on a computer, such as Windows, OS X, or Linux.

operator
A Scratch block that uses data to work something out, such as checking whether two values are equal or adding two numbers together.

output
Data that is produced by a computer program and viewed by the user.

pixel art
A drawing made of giant pixels or blocks, mimicking the appearance of graphics in early computer games.

pixels
The coloured dots on a screen that make up graphics.

procedure
Code that carries out a specific task, working like a program within a program. Also called a function, subprogram, or subroutine.

program
A set of instructions that a computer follows in order to complete a task.

programming language
A language that is used to give instructions to a computer.

project
Scratch's name for a program and all the assets that go with it.

random
A function in a computer program that allows unpredictable outcomes. Useful when creating games.

recursion
See *recursion*.

run
The command to make a program start.

Scratcher
Someone who uses Scratch.

script
A stack of instruction blocks under a header block that are run in order.

server
A computer that stores files accessible via a network.

software
Programs that run on a computer and control how it works.

sprite
A picture on the stage in Scratch that a script can move and change.

stage
The screen-like area of the Scratch interface in which projects runs.

statement
The smallest complete instruction a programming language can be broken down into.

string
A series of characters. Strings can contain numbers, letters, or symbols such as a colon.

subprogram or subroutine
Code that carries out a specific task, working like a program within a program. Also called a function or procedure.

variable
A place to store data that can change in a program, such as the player's score. A variable has a name and a value.

Index

D

dance mats **53**
dance-mat games 17, 53
"data" block 42, 43, 44, 197
debugging 46, **203**
"define" block 134, 173, 178
"delete this clone" block 79, 80, 113, 122
desktop computers 25
dice 39
difficulty level 13
  adjusting 47, 70–1, 86, 96, 125, 127, 163, 186, 202
  extra lives 126–7
directions **38**, 39
"division" block 187
Dog's Dinner **130–63**
  adding a character 142–4
  adding sound 144
  aim of the game 130–1
  bones for the dog 154–5
  creating a game control sprite 150–1
  drawing the platforms 148–9
  falling off the level 141
  fine-tuning 158–9
  fixing the jumping bugs 138–40
  hacks and tweaks 162–3
  hazardous food 157
  junk food 156
  making the levels 145–7
  placing the portals 152–3
  player on a platform 132–3
  running around 134–5
  signs and music 160–1
  up and down 136–8
Doom on the Broom **108–27**
  adding explosions 116–17
  aim of the game 108–9
  bat attack 114–15
  casting fireballs 113
  challenger mode 125
  controlling the witch 112
  extra lives hippo 126–7
  finishing touches 124–5
  fire-breathing dragon 120–1
  ghosts and ghouls 122–3
  hacks and tweaks 127
  setting the scene 110–11
  speedy spectre 118–19
double jump 141
drawing 210
designers *see* game designers
"duplicate" 67, 77

E

"early access" versions 213
enemies 12, 22
  adding 36, 38–9, 56, 64–5, 77, 111, 118–23
  better 44–5
  clones 81
  supernatural 122–3
"equal to" block 64
"equals" operator 82
eraser tool 60, 63
escape games 17
events **93**
Events blocks 93
events button 33
experimenting **22**
explosions 116–17

F

"Fall Speed" variable 98–9, 136, 139
"Fallen off" block 141
false statements 82
fill tool 61, 177
fine-tuning 46, 158–9, 186
  see also hacks and tweaks
fireworks 116–17
first-person games 187
fixed camera angle 187
flags 153
"Flip up-down" button 170
font size 69
"For all sprites" variable 193
"for" loops 78
"For this sprite only" variable 193
"forever" block 23, 32, 35
"forever" loops 52, 53, 64, 70, 78, 79
friends
  adding 77
  cloning 78–80
  extra lives 126–7
functions 134

G

game challenges 215
game clubs 215
Game Control sprite 150–1, 153, 159, 161, 162, 163
game design
  animation **111**

camera angles **187**
collision detection **143**
controllers **53**
designing levels **163**
from blocks to riches **213**
game physics **103**
game stories 14, **84**, 87
music **57**
the next level **210**
playability **13**
space **61**
virtual reality **15**
working with themes **121**
game designers 212
  learning from 210
game development **213**
game engines **211**
game idea generator **215**
game jams 214
Game Loop sprite 168, 176, 182, 185
game loops 168, **169**, 171, 172, 173
game over 66, 67, 69, 86, 96, 100–1, 124, 141, 162, 163, 168, 201, 202
game physics **103**, 211
game publishers 213
"Game Speed" variable 112, 125, 127
games
  atmosphere 14–15
  Cheese Chase **50–71**
  Circle Wars **74–87**
  creating your own 207
  debugging 46, **203**
  Dog's Dinner **130–63**
  fine-tuning 46, 158–9, 186
  Glacier Race **166–87**
  good ingredients 12–13
  how coding works 18–19
  improving your knowledge of 210
  jobs making games **212–13**
  Jumpy Monkey **90–105**
  planning a game 18
  playing 210
  Star Hunter **30–47**
  stories 14, **86**, 87
  testing 207
  Tropical Tunes **190–203**
  types of 16–17
gaming history 210
genres 16–17, 215
"ghost" block 152

ghosting 151
Glacier Race **166–87**
  adding obstacles 175–7
  adding sounds 174, 182, 185
  aims of the game 166–7
  collecting gems 180–2
  collisions and spins 174–7
  fine-tuning 186
  the game loop 168–9
  hacks and tweaks 186–7
  one-player version 186
  penguin in charge 182–5
  player two 177–9
  race cars 172–3
  scrolling road 170–1
"glide" blocks 45
global variables 193, 195, 196
"go to" blocks 40, 67, 70, 152, 155, 159, 178
"go to mouse-pointer" block 32, 77
"go to" trick **159**
goals 13, 210
goggles, virtual reality 15
graphics 15
graphics programs 209
gravity 90, 92, 95, 98–9, 136
  defying 103
  experimenting with 102–3
  real world **99**
  reverse 103, 163
"Gravity" variable 98, 102, 136, 163
"Grow" tool 76

H

hacks and tweaks
  Cheese Chase 70–1
  Circle Wars 86–7
  Dog's Dinner 162–3
  Doom on the Broom 127
  Glacier Race 186–7
  Jumpy Monkey 104–5
  Star Hunter 46–7
  Tropical Tunes 202
hardware 25
hazards 156–7
  adjusting speed of 163
Hazards sprite 157, 158, 162
health 12, 42
help tool 209
"hide" block 56, 85

Acknowledgments

Dorling Kindersley would like to thank: Bahja Norwood for editorial assistance and testing; Caroline Hunt for proofreading; and Helen Peters for the index.

Dorling Kindersley India would like to thank Riji Raju for editorial assistance.

Scratch is developed by the Lifelong Kindergarten Group at MIT Media Lab. See **http://scratch.mit.edu**